Reprints of Economic Classics

THE BRITISH WORKING CLASS READER

THE BRITISH
WORKING CLASS READER

1790-1848

LITERACY AND SOCIAL TENSION

BY

R. K. WEBB

[1955]

REPRINTS OF ECONOMIC CLASSICS

AUGUSTUS M. KELLEY · PUBLISHERS

NEW YORK 1971

First Edition 1955

(London: George Allen & Unwin Ltd., *Museum Street,*
1955)

Reprinted 1971 By
AUGUSTUS M. KELLEY · PUBLISHERS
New York New York 10001

By Arrangement With George Allen & Unwin Ltd.

I S B N 0 678 00578 8

L C N 55 27828

Printed in the United States of America
by Sentry Press, New York, N. Y. 10019

TO MY MOTHER

FOREWORD

FOREWORDS—and this one is no exception—serve to fore-warn the reader and to fore-arm the author, functions which, since the eighteenth century, the title-page can no longer adequately perform. Only the first chapter of this book deals in any general way with the working class reading public in Great Britain; there an assessment of literacy is made, and some of the types of reading to which they turned are indicated. The sub-title, *Literacy and Social Tension*, indicates the main concern of the study: the challenge which a literate working class presented to its betters.

For reasons explained in the text, many efforts to provide good or safe reading matter for the newly literate are passed over; attention is concentrated on areas of economic and social conflict, a choice of field which quite clearly dictates the limits in time, from the outbreak of the French Revolution to the relaxation of tension in the fifties. Within that field, representative attempts to deal with the problems raised will be presented. Newspaper writing is for the most part excluded, partly because of the dislocation of collections as a result of the war of 1939, partly because of the near impossibility of getting behind the anonymity of writing for the newspaper press. Of writers in periodicals and of books and pamphlets, some are included because their reputations demand it, some because they show the wide geographical and social spread of the responses. But the sampling is not entirely deliberate; some of it is dictated by the mere chance of survival of appallingly ephemeral literature.

In this field, too, class distinction is more important than it is in the rapidly expanding publication of fiction, cheap editions of the classics, or popularized science; for the ideas at stake here were ideas on which the ruling classes found themselves challenged, and for which they were compelled, either by fear or confidence, to demand or to persuade acceptance. The character of the ruling classes shifts during this half-century, and the new elements of British society which are associated in the work of government bring with them a full programme and a complete rationale. They found themselves in a class war—contemporaries had no doubt of that, however much they might try to explain it away. And their opponents were a broad grouping of types, levels, and occupations, blurring at the borderlines, even accepting some middle class cultural attributes, but, on the whole, distinct enough to permit the valid use of that conventional term, 'working class,' and to justify nineteenth-century statisticians in working out their proportion in the population.

The research on which this study is based was carried on over a two-year stay in Great Britain, made possible by the award of a Cutting Travelling Fellowship by Columbia University and by a grant under the Fulbright Act. To the University and to the staff of the United States Educational Commission in the United Kingdom I am very grateful. Publication has been assisted by a grant from the William A. Dunning Fund of the Department of History at Columbia. My heaviest indebtedness is to Professor J. B. Brebner, of Columbia University, and to Mr. H. L. Beales, of the London School of Economics and Political Science. I was able to draw on their friendship and wisdom on both sides of the Atlantic, and their criticism has saved me from many errors and the reader from more infelicities. For those which remain, the responsibility is mine alone.

For the use of manuscripts in their possession, I am deeply indebted to the Society for Promoting Christian Knowledge, London, and to University College, London. Especial thanks for the use of family papers and for their very kind hospitality are due to Mrs. R. S. Chambers, Balerno, Midlothian; Mr. A. S. Chambers, London; and Mr. C. W. Borlase Parker, Penzance.

The difficulty of searching out such obscure and forgotten materials as form the principal resources of this study meant a great reliance on the assistance and understanding of library staffs. The libraries in which I worked are listed in the note on sources. In addition, thanks are due to the Columbia University Library and the British Library of Political Science in the London School of Economics, where much of the groundwork of this book was laid. A particularly heavy debt is owed to the British Museum and to the Goldsmiths' Library of the University of London. All the librarians with whom I worked, and especially Mr. J. H. P. Pafford and his staff in the Goldsmiths' Library, contributed the most impressive proof that the eternal struggle between librarian and reader can be, no matter where the victory, not only bloodless but a positive pleasure.

R. K. W.

COLUMBIA UNIVERSITY
NEW YORK

CONTENTS

OF the working classes of Western Europe at least it may be pronounced certain, that the patriarchal or paternal system of government is one to which they will not again be subject. That question has been several times decided. It was decided when they were taught to read, and allowed access to newspapers and political tracts. It was decided when dissenting preachers were suffered to go among them, and appeal to their faculties and feelings in opposition to the creeds professed and countenanced by their superiors. It was decided when they were brought together in numbers, to work socially under the same roof. It was decided when railways enabled them to shift from place to place, and change their patrons and employers as easily as their coats. The working classes have taken their interests into their own hands, and are perpetually shewing that they think the interests of their employers not identical with their own, but opposite to them. Some among the higher classes flatter themselves that these tendencies may be counteracted by moral and religious education; but they have let the time go by for giving an education which can serve their purpose. The principles of the Reformation have reached as low down in society as reading and writing, and the poor will no longer accept morals and religion of other people's prescribing. I speak more particularly of our own country, especially the town population, and the districts of the most scientific agriculture and highest wages, Scotland and the north of England. . . .

It is on a far other basis that the well being and well doing of the labouring people must henceforth rest. The poor have come out of leading strings, and cannot any longer be governed or treated like children. To their own qualities must be commended the care of their destiny. . . . But whatever advice, exhortation, or guidance is held out to the labouring classes must henceforth be tendered to them as equals, and accepted with their eyes open. The prospect of the future depends on the degree in which they can be made rational beings.

JOHN STUART MILL
Principles of Political Economy (1848)

CHAPTER I

THE WORKING CLASS READING PUBLIC

1790–1848

In *Nightmare Abbey*, Peacock makes his reactionary Mr. Flosky lament: 'How can we be cheerful when we are surrounded by a *reading public*, that is growing too wise for its betters?' Unfair as a portrait of Coleridge, the character of Mr. Flosky is quite accurate as a type of his period, and not least so in expressing alarm about increasing literacy. In 1828 a barrister told the Westminster magistrates that a forger owed his trip to Botany Bay to the 'march of intellect,' and to this the magistrates (or some of them) responded with 'Hear, hear.'[1] Lord Eldon, according to Francis Place, considered the 'march of intellect . . . a tune to which one day or the other a hundred thousand tall fellows with clubs and pikes will march against Whitehall.'[2] The resurrection of these gentlemen, in an age so well supplied as ours with gloomy observers, would be an event welcome to few save historians; but, if Lord Eldon were to lecture today on the nineteenth century, he would certainly not list the creation of a reading public among the working classes as another baleful effect of the Education Act of 1870. That unfortunate development had come earlier.

Yet the idea persists that widespread literacy was an accomplishment of the late nineteenth century. A lack of statistics and an uncritical reliance on shocked statements of early Victorian reformers contribute to this belief. Again, our views may be too sophisticated. There are no tests and scales. One cannot even accept the popular definition of literacy as the ability to read and write, for writing in the nineteenth century was of much less importance than it is today. The inspectors' categories of those able to read and write, to read only, and to do neither, or of those unable and able to read 'an easy book,' are difficult or impossible to define. Their favourite criterion, the ability to read and explain a passage from the Bible, cannot stand up for a frightened child, or, indeed, for modern children more accustomed to testing. One must speak somewhat loosely for the nineteenth century, but it seems enough that a person had advanced sufficiently beyond a knowledge of his letters— this would certainly include most of the 'read only' or 'easy book' categories—to work through a handbill or a street ballad. Mr. Gamfield, the sweep, spelled through the bill offering the services of Oliver Twist.

It has been suggested that Tudor England may have known a literacy rate of forty or fifty per cent. and that a 'fair proportion' of the lower classes in the seventeenth century could read.[3] Such problems are outside the scope of this study, but it seems likely that, if the increasing education of the eighteenth century did no more than to hold ground already taken, the greater activity of the nineteenth century must have advanced from a relatively broad base.

The spread of education was the outcome of a number of motives, one or another of which might appeal to most groups in the country. First, there was the religious impulse. The wish of George III that every child in his kingdoms might learn to read the Bible struck a most responsive chord in his philanthropic subjects. High Church, Methodism, and Evangelicalism all contributed, and even among the sceptics the importance of learning to read the Bible was stressed.

Closely connected with religion was the maintenance of the social order and a due subordination and respect to superiors and to the laws of society. Eldon and the Wiltshire farmer who suggested restricting the teaching of reading and writing to the children whose parents could guarantee their future behaviour were a declining breed.[4] Some enthusiasts, to be sure, had only a limited education in mind. Patrick Colquhoun, for example, made it very clear that the minds of the poor should not be elevated above their station, and that schemes for an extensive diffusion of knowledge were utopian, injurious, and absurd.[5]

Others pointed out that an extended education, while it might conceivably lead young persons astray, could lead them also to books which would defeat the enemies of society.[6]

Brougham maintained that the education of the poor was 'the best security for the morals, the subordination, and the peace of countries'; and Southey, too, called for an educated population, fed with the milk of sound doctrine.[7] By the forties opinion had so far broadened that Samuel Smiles could welcome an education which would increase self-respect and ambition, no matter whom it disturbed. 'The real danger is, in excess of ignorance, not in excess of knowledge; in the blind groping in darkness, and not in the light which illumines every nook and cranny of the social edifice.'[8]

The appearance of wide statistical inquiries stimulated much upper class activity. Literacy figures for criminals were endlessly debated, but the victory seemed to fall to the side represented by John Clay, the chaplain of the Preston House of Correction. Education, he maintained, prevented crime either by inculcating religious principles or by creating tastes incompatible with the 'low and debasing propensities' which led the ignorant and sensual to violate the laws.[9] Similarly, a scarcity of truly educated persons in workhouses was made to argue for education, overlooking a possible confusion of cause and effect.[10]

While reasons such as these led the upper classes to found and encourage schools, other factors sent the working classes to them, for short periods at any rate. Those whose economic position was improving—their number was steadily increasing —could find the money for fees and sent their children quite without philanthropic urging.[11] As the ability to read spread, so did its value in social prestige, and the desire to have one's children in school and well-dressed became increasingly effective. The industrial system put a premium on literacy, as it demanded skills and responsibilities, while crowding into cities developed new challenges and problems. Working families might well have sent their children to a dame to get them out of the way or to be kept while the mother worked. The influence of the crises of the period—bringing a new play of ideas, class-consciousness, and constant prescriptions of most working-class leaders to 'get knowledge'—must have been potent, if immeasurable.[12]

Two sets of motives, then, working from different directions, caused schools to be set up and children to be sent to them. What were the schools? First of all, the great variety of charity schools, dating from the end of the seventeenth century and the beginning of the eighteenth, many of which survived into the nineteenth century, to become the aristocracy of schools for the lower orders.[13] Next in point of time, and perhaps of more importance, were the Sunday schools. A major form of charitable activity from the middle of the eighteenth century, they were oriented to a segment of the population untouched by the charity schools, whose numbers and accommodation were limited. Their foundation was helped on by a rapidly growing Sabbatarianism. A guess at the actual attendance in the thirties was hazarded at 800,000 to 900,000, a quite remarkable figure.[14]

Most Sunday schools taught little more than reading. Indeed, in some schools, anything beyond reading was held in abhorrence. Hannah More assured her bishop in 1801 that she would 'allow of no writing for the poor,' and twenty years later she was trying to prevail on parliamentary friends 'to steer the middle way between the scylla of brutal ignorance and the charybdis of a literary education,' the one cruel, the other preposterous.[15] There were exceptions, however, and some Sunday schools held evening sessions to teach writing and arithmetic. Apparently dissenting Sunday schools were far ahead of Church schools in teaching such 'secular' subjects.[16]

There is considerable testimony to the effectiveness of Sunday schools, which cannot be ignored. In parts of the country they were the only means of education, in others the principal means. A witness before the Education Committee in 1835 stated that Sunday schools had not been given sufficient credit; he lamented that boys left the schools so early, but he thought that they stayed long enough to get a competent knowledge of reading. Frederic Hill, at about the same time, recognized that, while for some children the degree of attainment was slight enough to prevent pleasure in reading, 'thousands and tens of thousands' of the working classes, including most of the potential leaders, had learned to read fluently in Sunday schools.[17]

The day school situation is appallingly confused. Pride of place goes invariably to the schools of the two great societies, the British and Foreign School Society and the National

Society for Educating the Poor according to the Principles of the Established Church, each with a tutelary genius—Joseph Lancaster and Andrew Bell respectively—each with wide philanthropic support and eventually increasing government subsidies, and each with allegiance to its own form of the incredibly cheap, attractive, and abominable monitorial system, in which older children taught the younger. These schools spread rapidly. The National Society, for example, in 1813 had 230 schools, with 40,484 scholars, day and Sunday; in 1820 there were 1,614 schools, with about 200,000 scholars; and in 1830, 3,670 schools with about 346,000 scholars.[18] But for all the attention the method got, even from Jeremy Bentham, the schools were certainly not so effective as they should have been. A shortage of teachers and the irregular attendance of pupils combined with the defects of the system to prevent little more acquisition than a knowledge of reading, and that was often imperfect. At the Borough Road School, the model establishment of the British and Foreign Society, the average attendance was not over thirteen months. The master indicated that children remaining twelve months would have learned to read, while those remaining three or four years would have learned to read and write well, to do simple sums, and to make some acquaintance with geography and geometry. But those children were very few.[19]

Other types of schools supplemented the work of the great societies. Workhouse schools and schools of industry undoubtedly served some purpose in the inculcation of factory discipline, but, educationally, did little more than impart a faulty ability to read.[20] Backwaters of neglect were discovered and schools founded to cope with them; hence organizations like the Children's Friend Society and the Ragged School Union.[21] Factory owners also set to educating, more or less, the children they employed, either on their own initiative or through pressure brought by the new factory inspectors and good employers. The Chartist outbreaks of 1839 convinced some employers of the wisdom of providing some sort of instruction as insurance; and examples throughout Britain, in all types of manufacturing and mining, can be easily found.

Particularly useful in studying factory schools are the reports of H. S. Tremenheere, who became an educational inspector in 1839 and inspector of mining areas under Lord Ashley's Act of 1842.[22] For example, he reported from Lanarkshire that the Messrs. Baird found that not only were the children beneficiaries of instruction and supervision, but that parents as well were 'led insensibly to better habits by observing the effects of the school upon their children.'[23]

But all was not so easy. Not only were there bad employers, who could undercut more philanthropic competitors; there were also refractory and suspicious parents. Perhaps, some of them thought, the masters had a sinister object behind all these libraries and schools; and, indeed, when one proprietor of an iron works offered to pay twopence a week for any of the children of his employees, about fifteen hundred in number, whom they would send to school, only thirty parents accepted the offer. Miners frequently preferred to send their children to old-fashioned schools, particularly the Sunday schools of the dissenters and Methodists.[24]

Finally, one other type of school must be mentioned, the 'adventure school' or 'dame school,' started by private individuals in response to a demand not otherwise met. They became very common in the eighteenth century, and by 1801 Mrs. Trimmer, the Anglican tract-writer, could assert, with probably not too much hyperbole, that 'every town and most villages' were sufficiently supplied with such elementary teaching. Frequently, no doubt, these schools were very bad, but a perceptive modern writer has suggested that, during their ascendancy and in rude surroundings, they filled adequately a clear need; while in towns where the demand was of superior quality, there were many instances of success. 'The confession elicited from the dames at a later date—"it's little they pays us, and it's little we teaches them"—is the perennial murmur of protectionists in the declining years of an industry whose profits and whose fame are gone.'[25]

It has been calculated that in 1833 the working class population of England and Wales numbered about 12,400,000, of whom 2,604,000 were between the ages of three and twelve. By correcting the deficient figures submitted to Parliament in 1833, an estimate of nearly 900,000 working class children in attendance at school in that year has been reached, a figure nearly doubled by 1851.[26] But a child was rarely expected to be in school before the age of five or after the age of ten or eleven, so that 2,000,000 might be a safer base. Further, the figures do not include Sunday schools, nor do they give sufficient weight to the remarkable turnover in attendance, which probably means that a much larger proportion of children of the working classes had some experience in schools than has been thought or than can be proved statistically.

In Scotland there were three distinct educational situations. In the lowland rural parishes, the strong tradition of parochial and burghal schools continued, supplemented, as the system ossified, by private adventure schools like that of Nanse Banks and Sabrina Hooky in John Galt's *Annals of the Parish*. There, for the most part, education was universal and effective, and it was to this aspect of Scottish education that reformers south of the Tweed referred with admiration and envy. The Highlands, however, were badly handicapped by language, geography, poverty, and neglect; and it was only in the first decades of the nineteenth century that a spate of philanthropic enterprise made significant inroads on the ignorance of that remote part of the world. The worst situation was undoubtedly in the towns, where rapid industrialization brought problems of overcrowding and squalour which pretty well defied charitable activity. Despite the expedients of sessional and Sunday schools and other schemes, primarily religious, the large towns educationally were no better than their counterparts to the south, if indeed they came up even to that standard.[27]

Obviously, in so varied and inefficient an educational structure as that which has been sketched, children did not acquire a great deal, probably little more than some ability to read. Quite aside from the dubious quality of the teaching, there was the problem of attendance. Tremenheere asserted in mid-century that nowhere in the coal and iron districts would a child have to go farther from home than a mile to find a 'creditable or even a good school,' but that parents were disinclined to permit their children to stay long enough to obtain any real benefit. Certainly by 'real benefit' he did not mean mere reading, for that ability alone led such young men as could read to read only 'trash.' Complaints of that nature are frequent. For example, a Scottish investigator in 1819-20 lamented that, of those who could read, 'few had recourse to the books calculated to give them the most useful instruction, because they were unable to understand the language; while most resorted to works of a lighter and unfortunately less exceptionable kind, which they found it not so difficult to comprehend.'[28] But, for the less idealistic purposes of this study, it is quite enough that young men were enabled to read 'trash,' for 'trash' in the nineteenth century was a very inclusive term. The serious allegations that, once out of school, young people lost their imperfectly acquired skill, may appear less formidable, if the estimates of literacy shortly to be made are considered along with evidence of an ever-present opportunity and encouragement to read, at least in the towns. The same factor palliates the charge of inspectors that the schools failed to make children understand what they read. High standards, nineteenth century or modern, cannot apply; Bible and Catechism are not handbills and last dying speeches.[29]

For the upper levels of the working classes, it is not enough to refer simply to schools, for this was the century of Samuel Smiles and self-help; and the exertions of isolated individuals, reports of whose exploits in self-education have survived to amaze a less devoted age, cannot have been so isolated after all. In the forties the Leeds Mutual Improvement Society was founded by four young workmen, and meetings were held in an old garden house to which young men came to learn to read for a subscription of threepence a week. At about the same time reading rooms were set up by artisans in Hampstead. Small reading and study groups continually crop up in radical and trade union history, while Methodist class meetings often developed into little informal schools. The co-operative movement in its earliest days had plans for educating children of its members in co-operative Sunday schools and informal neighbourhood groups.[30] There were even more humble levels— teaching to read by members of the family, fellow apprentices, or friends. James Lackington, the bookseller, recalled that he forgot what he learned from the dame; but, when he was bound apprentice and stimulated by discussion, he started to read again through instruction by his employer's wife and youngest son, a boy of fourteen, to whom he paid three half-pence for an hour's lesson. And in Scotland, where inability to read must have been a real disgrace, there are references to the prevalence of private and imperfect teaching by relatives and friends, or—how tantalizing the suggestion is—'by boys proceeding from house to house.'[31]

Now that the variety of means by which members of the working classes could learn to read has been sketched, it is possible to turn to a statistical examination of working class literacy. For the earlier part of the century there is little information, but an enquiry at the end of the Napoleonic wars is worth noting. One John Freeman visited 153 families and found 594 persons, including 268 children. Of the adults, 216 were able to read and 110 were illiterate. Believing this proportion to be fair, he transferred it to the population of England in the 1811 census and calculated that 1,759,148 adults were unable to read, as against 3,454,327 literate adults. Other calculations were applied, and he ended by admitting a lack of evidence; yet he could not conclude, under the circumstances, 'that, in this kingdom, there are less than twelve hundred thousand persons to whom a Bible is useless, in consequence of their incapacity to read.'[32] He did not specify the location of his samples, nor the classes included in them; but the proportion of two-thirds literate should be borne in mind.

The statistical situation improved markedly in the thirties, and for the crucial years from 1832 to 1848 one can form some fairly reliable opinions. Most writers have depended on figures for educational attainments of criminals, which began to be published by the Home Office in 1835, or on the reports of the Registrar-General from 1837 of the number of signatures put to marriage registers. Both are faulty indices. On the face of it, figures relying on the criminal group exclusively should be too low for the overwhelmingly large respectable working class; while a number of objections can be brought against equating ability to read with ability to write, not the least of which is the disparity in the facilities for learning and using the two skills. Reports of inspectors, testimony in parliamentary investigations, and enquiries by the new statistical societies provide better guides, though samples are small and common denominators non-existent.[33] One thing is certain: the variation displayed in the country was astounding, variation even from parish to parish, depending on factors of geography, migration, and the incidence of philanthropy.

Yet, for all the variation, there are some amazing consistencies. There is a continual recurrence of a proportion of two to one or three to two for the ability to read and the ability to write; likewise there is, among different occupational groups, and different areas, and among reports whose accuracy was affirmed and reports whose accuracy was doubted, a hovering about the figures of two-thirds to three-quarters literate, for working classes alone. Perhaps the figure, insofar as one dares attempt an over-all estimate in view of the local variation, should be nearer the latter proportion than the former.[34] Available estimates, even in southern agricultural districts, certainly among the worst, rarely dropped much below fifty per cent.; and, indeed, the indignation of writers grew very warm when that figure was reached. There were, to be sure, isolated instances in parishes or in collieries where the literacy rate was much below fifty per cent., but there were certainly parishes and collieries which more than balanced the bad figures. As one advances from south to north, a greater consciousness of the value of education seems prevalent, and the high figures in some northern colliery areas, plus the fairly consistent figures for large industrial centres, probably incline the balance to the higher end of the scale.[35] It must be said also that, of the one-quarter to one-third of the working class population remaining totally illiterate, a large part must have been among the very lowest levels, a fact which would correspondingly raise the literacy of the body of workmen who made up the great political potential in English life.

In rural parishes of lowland Scotland, as comments sprinkled through the *New Statistical Account* indicate, illiteracy was all but unknown; but the deficiency in schools in the Highlands and towns indicated earlier meant a bad showing in literacy in these areas. Variation again was great. In the Orkneys and Shetlands, early in the twenties, only 12 per cent. were unable to read, while the west coast and outer islands ran as high as 70 per cent. illiterate. The Highlands, however, are of little concern in this study, because the complications of language created a separate problem, and because the great clearances and consequent emigration both absorbed attention and removed much of the population from the predominantly political questions which are important here. The towns, on the other hand, are of very great importance. Here there were striking differentiations among occupations, even within the same factory, with highly skilled or carefully regulated groups much more literate than their less skilled or less prosperous fellows. The decline in education among the handloom weavers is especially striking. Towns like Dundee and Paisley were apparently much better off in education than Glasgow and Edinburgh; and, for a general estimate, it would seem to be justifiable to assume a sort of parity with industrial towns under similar conditions in England.[36]

The certainty of the existence of a working class reading public is plain. Mr. Flosky's lamentations seem to be justified both by the scale and variety of educational provision and by statistical investigation. It is also certain, despite the pitfalls of generalization in a situation which defies it, that that reading public was very probably much larger than has been generally thought. To be sure, it was a reading public with limitations. Reading was not always easy, and it was probably not habitual. Standards must be low, and one must be wary of denunciations of 'trash.' In many ways, it was a *potential* reading public, yet there existed many opportunities to read and to improve one's skill. Any estimation of the political and social implications of this new phenomenon must be considered in the light of the fantastic multiplication of all kinds of printed material, and the remainder of this chapter will be devoted to a cursory examination of the types of reading matter which encouraged many to read and which formed the great bulk of the reading of most of the literate working classes.

It is necessary to stop first to indicate two easily forgotten factors. First, there was the appearance of new forms of lighting which made reading on long evenings a more comfortable and rewarding procedure, especially in the towns, where one could make use of reading rooms more pleasant than drab overcrowded homes. Second, there was a great provision of reading matter which by no stretch of the imagination could be called literary.

Here the controlling factor was price and, for the most part, a tax-induced price. Many tradesmen used discarded books and newspapers to replace expensive wrapping paper,[37] so printed matter came into the hands of nearly everyone. As late as the thirties of the nineteenth century, one enthusiastic and almost too typical Scot saw a way to the 'unlimited diffusion of useful knowledge at no expense to the reader,' in associating the cultivation of the intellect with the necessaries of life. For a trifling expense, blank papers, wrappers, and the reverse side of handbills could be printed with, say, 'an interesting account of the culture of tea, sugar, tobacco, etc., with instructions for using them in the best and most economical manner, and for discriminating good and bad qualities. . . .' Advertising too would be promoted, for newspaper notices were necessarily brief and ephemeral, while by this means, 'circulars, shop-bills, and tracts, might be easily rendered interesting and instructive, and would be therefore anxiously sought after, read, and preserved.'[38] Modern manufacturers, at any rate, have followed a similar course, and anyone who has seen a child reading the tales and puffery on a cereal package or who can remember doing it himself, can hardly afford to scoff at the suggestion or the process.

Advertising was driven by heavy duties from the newspapers into the streets. Walls, vehicles, shop-windows, newspaper offices, and bookstalls made the streets a sort of poor man's library.[39] Educational reformers were concerned. Thomas Wyse, parliamentary spokesman for the Central Society of Education, was convinced in the late thirties that town residents did not forget what they had learned in school because handbills and placards and other objects continually demanded the use of reading ability. 'The walls of a town often exhibit the worst kind of schoolbook for young or old.'[40] And in Harriet Martineau's *Scholars of Arneside* occurs a conversation which must reflect a reality:

'There is one thing easy to see,' observed Jay, the builder; 'and that is the figure that people make of our walls, sticking them all over with bills. I have more trouble than enough with pulling them down from the end of my master's house; and as sure as I next pass that way, I find it all covered over again with red and black letters, and ugly pictures. . . .'
Ambrose stood up for the practice of plastering the walls with bills; he having been often amused, and even led to read, by a tempting display of this kind. But it did not take

long to convince him that he might be better amused and
more comfortably advanced in his reading, if he could but
be supplied at his own home with a sufficiency of pictures
and articles to study.[41]

Again it must be remembered that a modern child very early
goes to school to trams and hoardings.

In turning to the literary output directed to mass circulation,
attention is first required for a class of publications, widely
publicized and praised, which will receive scant treatment in
this study; but, in passing, a tentative assessment of its importance must be made. The output of the religious press from
the end of the eighteenth century was enormous. Mrs. Sarah
Trimmer, for example, concerned about the developing ability
to read, and even more anxious about the fate of the Establishment, started in the eighties publications to provide the poor
with safe reading. *The Family Magazine* was intended to instruct
and amuse cottagers and servants, especially through instructive tales, later published separately, 'designed to convey to
the lower orders of the people many instructive lessons, and
also to point out to their superiors the proper manner of
treating them, in order to correct many of the faults peculiar
to their humble station in life.'[42] Mrs. Trimmer's works had
a high reputation among evangelical churchmen and were
important enough to gain Cobbett's denunciation. Similarly,
Hannah More and her sisters and friends devoted themselves
to tract publication, their most remarkable effort being the
Cheap Repository Tracts of the mid-nineties,[43] intended to
answer Voltaire and Paine, to counteract French Revolutionary
ideas, and to promote a proper regard for the social order.
Hannah More was certain that one ballad had prevented a riot
among colliers near Bath, when a gentleman caused it to be
distributed and sung. Another, teaching acceptance of the
wrongs of this world as part of a divine plan, gave the reader,
said the Bishop of London, 'Bishop Butler's Analogy, all for
a halfpenny.'[44]

Serious efforts were made to adapt such publications to
what the popular taste was, or was believed to be. Collections
of popular literature were made to serve as models, and the
tracts were published with eye-catching titles and suggestive

woodcuts to attract readers who might, it must be said, be disappointed, once they had sampled the hygienic contents. Efforts were made to investigate the hawkers' trade and to get the tracts into their hands for distribution. And upper class support was heavily relied upon. But it would seem that the distribution was not always so effective as the promoters had hoped. At any rate, the Bishop of London suggested the adoption in London of a Manchester scheme for distribution to charity children, who might in turn supply their parents, 'and thus get them introduced among a greater number of the lower class than we have yet been able to do.' Francis Place indicated years later that the tracts circulated chiefly in the rural districts, where upper class pressure would have had greater effect.[45]

Religious publication was, above all, a field for the activity of societies. Although the Society for Promoting Christian Knowledge had, like the rest of the Establishment, remained fairly somnolent during most of the eighteenth century, in the nineteenth it was forced to action by the impact of events, and set to circulating not only religious works, but some dealing with political and social matters. More instructive is the Religious Tract Society, founded in 1799. It was generally approved by the piety of the times, and in 1842 its tract publication produced a profit of three thousand pounds.[46] Here too considerable effort was devoted to the problem of pitching the tracts on the right level to appeal to the potential audience. In 1805 attempts were made to draw away the trade of the 'vile publications' sold by hawkers,[47] but the hawkers were not a successful outlet; rather the Society had to depend on free distribution by enthusiastic individuals or groups. The poor avoided buying tracts, but the sales to the upper classes were very large. The tract tradition was a strong one in the nineteenth century. Servants' halls were supplied with them by benevolent or worried masters; visitors regularly left tracts on their calls, while gifts of food to the poor did not neglect spiritual nourishment tucked away in the baskets.[48] One clergyman in Sussex commended the example of a gentleman who sought out the hawkers in his neighbourhood, bought up all their stock, and sent them off to a bookseller's shop in Hastings where they would be supplied free with tracts and

children's books. All the offers were 'thankfully accepted.'
Another suggestion made strongly in the Society's journal
was the distribution of tracts at executions, where one could
find hundreds of the most degraded of the lower orders 'not
commonly accessible to Christian effort.' At one execution
42,575 tracts were given away; at another, 40,850! Attempts to
mimic broadsides and last dying speeches, however, proved un-
successful, and the Society 'reluctantly' abandoned the effort.[49]

There were many other societies active in the field, and
when the Whigs talked down the menace of seditious and
infidel literature, they cited the vast circulation of religious
publications. Yet it seems probable that the success of these
efforts was less than has been commonly supposed. A committee investigating Westminster schools found not a single
publication of the R.T.S. and only one instance of the use of the
Saturday Magazine of the S.P.C.K. It was the impression of the
agents in another investigation in the east end of London that,
of all the books found—and more than one-quarter of the
houses were without any serious books at all—the Bible and
Testament were least read. Tracts might be read once, or not
read at all and thrown away. They might be preserved simply
for the inspection of the clergyman or the visitor on his subsequent rounds. And, being paper, an immensely large number
of tracts must have gone to light fires or to serve baser but
vital domestic purposes which religious writers would understandably not care to mention.[50] There are also indications of
a fifth column. Infidel distributors, alleged the *Christian Spectator*,
put 'Socinian, or Infidel, or Popish tracts' in R.T.S. covers,
and one Manchester radical undertook to answer all the tracts
left him by writing in blank spaces 'some very pithy political
or philosophical sentence,' and so making them 'subservient
to a purpose diametrically opposite to their intention, namely,
the diffusion of truth.'[51]

The future historian of the Religious Tract Society, in a
prize essay in 1850, cited figures to show how much greater
was the circulation of the unstamped press on the side of
'moral corruption' than that of the entire religious output.
Further, religious literature circulated chiefly among 'professing
Christians of the middle classes'; while the more unsavoury
sheets found their way, 'in very large proportion, to the homes

and haunts of the poor.' Distribution was faulty, for one thing; secularist publications gave a profit of 42 per cent., religious publications only 25 per cent., with the result that back street bookshops were filled with Reynolds and Cleave and excluded the Tract Society. But the principal difficulty was one of tone and style. Infidel publications showed a real knowledge of the people for whom they were intended; that could be said of no religious publication. Their 'inflexible style of phraseology, together with the uniform mould of thought, impart a technical, exclusive character, to the whole teaching, and effectually bar its access to any mind unfamiliar with the dialect of the sanctuary.'[52]

Tract writers, then, were faced with the same problems as were other writers for the lower classes; like most of them, they failed to solve them, and so, in large part, failed in their greater mission. Religious publications are clearly important as a nineteenth century phenomenon; but they were apparently read largely by the already pious middle classes and failed to convert the unconverted. As a significant social agency among the working classes, their effectiveness may have been pretty well limited, like advertisements or the publications they set out to replace, to providing some practice in reading, but, unlike the latter, practice usually quite devoid of entertainment.

The successful distributors were clearly the hawkers and the 'back street booksellers,' and it is important to survey the kinds of publications which they sold. One very popular item was the almanac. The stamped almanacs of the Stationers' Company were, however, attacked by reformers. The *Athenaeum* in 1828 called them 'vaporous modifications of palpable imposture, impudent mendacity, vulgar ignorance, and low obscenity,' and went on to point out that, although they were a type of publication more than any other consulted daily by persons of every level, they had not changed in nature since witches were burnt and horoscopes drawn. Three scientific almanacs circulated about 4,000; two professional almanacs (both clerical), about 3,500; sheet almanacs for business purposes, 50,000; harmless pocket books, 20,000; but the popular and astrological or obscene almanacs—*Moore's, Moore's Improved, John Partridge's, Poor Robin's,* and *Seasar on the Seasons*—sold 500,000![53]

Yet this remarkable figure does not take into account the sale of unstamped almanacs; in 1821, only one person in forty bought a stamped almanac—the duty was one shilling and threepence—and prosecutions for the sale of the unstamped variety paralleled the prosecutions against vendors of unstamped newspapers.[54] Charles Knight, touring the manufacturing districts for the Society for the Diffusion of Useful Knowledge, reported that scarcely a cottage was without an unstamped sheet called 'The Tradesman's and Farmer's Calendar,' containing information peculiar to the area. The proprietor lived in Bolton, and, prior to the publication of the regular almanacs, sent his agents to every market within fifty miles, where the sheet, called a 'paddy,' sold at threepence or fourpence. A bookseller in Nottingham affirmed that 20,000 were sold there.[55] The popularity of almanacs is emphasized by their use as devices to propagandize some particular cause. One almanac was commended to 'real radical reformers' by Henry Hunt in 1834; the corn law struggle had its almanacs; Van Diemen's Land sent almanacs to England which were undoubtedly used in the drive to encourage emigration. And very nearly the first thing to which the Society for the Diffusion of Useful Knowledge turned its attention was the publication of the *British Almanac*. Supplemented by a *Companion*, it was probably the most successful, if among the least publicized, of the Society's publications.[56]

The great bulk of popular literature handled by hawkers and booksellers was that known in the earlier period as chapbooks, a typical eighteenth-century form of publication. Usually the term calls to mind a tiny leaflet of sixteen or twenty-four pages, execrably printed on poor paper and illustrated with a crude wood-cut, and sold at prices ranging from a farthing to a shilling. These leaflets often contained tales or histories, but the category also includes broadsides and slips carrying ballads, scandal, accounts of executions and last dying speeches. The tone of chapbook literature did not set well with the more prudish nineteenth century; hence the denunciations of the hawkers' baskets already encountered. The tales were usually humorous, and the humour was likely to be very earthy. Plots might be borrowed or taken from folk tradition; but the really good writers, able to give an intense local flavour, saw clearly into the needs of an audience seeking relaxation or compensation in these simple tales.[57]

London was the great centre, but in many ways provincial production is more striking. Any printer out of his indentures, who could get some paper and an old worn font of type might set up in the business, which was apparently steady and not unremunerative. Thus, the firm of Cheney in Banbury in the 1790's carried on a small chapbook business in addition to regular job work; the annual turnover in chapbooks in 1812-20 was £338. Their chapbook trade died out after 1820, only a broadside of 1822 and a political ballad of 1832 remaining in existence today; but an inventory of 1808-20 shows seventy-five titles. The Harvard catalogue lists seventy-four places of publication in Great Britain and Ireland, a remarkable number in view of the unlikelihood of survival and Atlantic crossing. Indeed, it seems possible that chapbook publishing was so widespread that a firm could exist simply to supply woodcuts. Scotland was a particularly active area, probably in part because of the wider extent of literacy in the country; and many Scottish chapbooks were pirated south of the border, particularly in Newcastle, which, next to London, was the largest centre for their production.[58]

It is usual to speak of the disappearance of the chapbook in the first half of the nineteenth century, or at any rate of its retreat into more remote districts; it has also been customary to ascribe this disappearance to the provision of a more wholesome literature for the poor by the Chambers brothers, Charles Knight, and others.[59] An assessment of these publications will be made later, and the whole problem of popular literature in the thirties and forties awaits a close study; but it seems possible here to hazard a guess that the change in popular literature—neither so great nor so cataclysmic as has been implied—was due rather to the mechanization of the industry and the improvement of transport which facilitated the expansion and centralization of newspapers, magazines, serial stories, and novels in parts; and to the increasing ability in and habit of reading which made the cruder and simpler tales of an earlier generation fall away.

Certainly the execution broadside did not disappear, and the ballad business continued to flourish. The Birmingham

Reference Library contains a fine collection of nineteenth century execution slips, including one as late as 1877, and an advertisement for a ballad welcoming Garibaldi to England, published by W. S. Fortey of Seven Dials, 'the oldest and cheapest house in the world for ballads (4,000 sorts).' Mayhew's investigations in London in the late forties turned up some amazing information: 2,500,000 copies were printed of sheets on the Rush and Manning executions, over a million and a half each on several others; most of the printing was centralized in London. 'Cocks'—sheets on elopements, love letters, and so on—printed nearly 3,500 copies weekly in the metropolis. A vendor told of making fifteen shillings on a Saturday night and Sunday morning selling odd numbers of periodicals, tales, and the like for a master whose weekend sales may have reached ten thousand. The business, he said, fell off after 'the periodicals came so low and so many on 'em, that they wouldn't sell at all.'[60] And of the periodicals, police reports were important components, lamented by some, praised by a few. Cleave's famous radical paper was the *Police Gazette*; Hetherington's *Twopenny Dispatch* was also a police gazette.

The craze for cheap fiction is the outstanding characteristic of popular literature, and by mid-century the magazines which catered to it had enormous circulations. Cheap novels were published in penny or twopenny volumes or numbers—the distinction from the older chapbooks perhaps not so clear—both in London and in the provinces.[61] Upper class concern over such reading habits was very great, and their indignation was visited especially on the sensational publications of G. W. M. Reynolds and Edward Lloyd, chief of the 'Salisbury Square School of Fiction.' Perhaps no better explanation of the popularity and real importance of this literature can be found than Dickens's impatient reply to Charles Knight's complaints about its hold on the public:

The English are, so far as I know, the hardest worked people on whom the sun shines. Be content if in their wretched intervals of leisure they read for amusement and do no worse. They are born at the oar, and they live and die at it. Good God, what would we have of them![62]

This survey of working class reading must conclude with some discussion of the form of publication which was the most significant enthusiasm of this new reading public, and which provides the transition to the main concern of this book. There was much eighteenth-century comment on the influence and extent of the newspaper.[63] But, however great its importance may have seemed to contemporaries, the fact remains that the role of the regular newspaper was strictly limited throughout the eighteenth century and well into the nineteenth. Basically, it was a matter of expense. The price of paper was high and raised still higher by taxation; printing, by hand presses until the second and third decades of the new century, was relatively slow and restricted output. The price was further and intentionally increased by the stamp duty. That meant that after 1815 papers, limited to one sheet—four pages—crammed with advertisements and compressed statements of the news, sold for the usual price of sevenpence a copy, certainly prohibitive, on other than a club basis, to any below the ranks of the well-to-do. Sales were low. Three London newspapers sold as many as three thousand stamped copies a day in 1821; and only weeklies existed outside of London; the total weekly sale was only half a million.[64]

Yet the craze for newspapers grew rapidly. A writer in Knight's *London* playfully referred to the newspaper as more indispensable to the Englishman than his teakettle. Knight himself testified to their importance by founding the *Companion to the Newspaper*, to comment from a moderate middle-class point of view on current events; while Brougham lamented that the 'taxes on knowledge' prevented the Society for the Diffusion of Useful Knowledge from 'wrapping up good information of a lasting value in news,' which might have increased the popularity of its publications.[65]

Until the stamp duty was lowered to a penny in 1836, the principal resource of the working man was the unstamped press, which so alarmed the respectable classes and the government. But there were ways and means of getting at even the expensive sheets, and the ingenuity displayed is probably the most eloquent comment on the popularity of the newspaper among the lower classes. The hiring out of papers was illegal after 1789, but the ban was apparently of little account. John

Cleave in the thirties advertised the *Times*, *Morning Chronicle*, and *True Sun* for sale, post free, at half price, on the second day of publication. Crowds collected before the windows of newspaper offices where the latest sheet was displayed, and newspapers passed from hand to hand. It has been calculated that London papers were read by thirty persons, provincial papers by eight to thirty. These journals were, of course, printed on rag paper and so could stand up to much more handling than modern papers.[66]

The public house, the beer shop, and the coffee house were places where newspapers might be read. Cooke Taylor in the forties found that in Manchester the newspaper was frequently the chief attraction in public houses, particularly on Sundays. In London the *Morning Advertiser* was the public house journal, and, after a copy was stale in the pub, it might circulate through an entire street, families having arranged with the potboy for an hour's loan of it. It was this paper, interestingly enough, that Marx chose as a vehicle for his controversy in the fifties.[67] Coffee houses were increasing rapidly in the metropolis during these years—at the end of the forties there were estimated to be 888 of them, as against 5,260 pubs and 2,748 beer shops— and testimony before a parliamentary committee in 1840 discloses the extent to which some of them served as reading rooms for working men. One proprietor, for example, whose house was in High Holborn, paid out, prior to the reduction of the stamp tax, four hundred pounds a year for newspapers, magazines, and the binding of back numbers. Lovett and Cleave both opened coffee houses and advertised the large numbers of periodicals which they took in.[68] The *Pioneer* for 10 May, 1834, contains a letter from 'One of the Unwashed,' who had a quarrel with the *Times*; he suggested a boycott of the *Times* by the '1,000 or so "humble" coffee houses in and about London,' nearly all of which took in the paper; and he cited an example where the workmen of a cabinet factory had got it turned out of four eating houses and four coffee houses. The prospectus of J. S. Buckingham's evening paper, the *Argus*, pointed out as one of its virtues that each number could be separated into inner and outer pages, each with its own department of information, and so capable of serving two readers at once, 'so as to make it especially convenient for

Families, Clubs, Libraries, Reading-Rooms, Taverns, Coffee-Houses, and all other places of public resort. . . .'[69]

Finally, in any estimate of the newspaper audience, it must be emphasized that it extended far beyond the limits of the reading public. There was also a hearing public. Place pointed out that it was not uncommon for the men in a workshop engaged in quiet employment, such as tailoring, to commission one man to read aloud, while the others worked, doing his work as compensation. A letter in *Chambers's Journal* describes a similar procedure in hackling shops in Dundee and elsewhere; each shop took a local and a London, Edinburgh, and Glasgow paper; each man read his share; and the papers were re-sold for at least two-thirds of their value, sometimes to workmen to read to their families, sometimes to send on to distant friends.[70] Methodist, radical, Chartist, and self-improvement classes and meetings often included reading aloud as a feature; it was certainly done in homes where perhaps only one member of the family could read; and Tremenheere was alarmed by a Primitive Methodist preacher's reading the *Northern Star* weekly at a miners' meeting. And this too was a feature of public house life. The *Spectator* reported that

> in most towns of the kingdom, there are public-houses, the landlords of which retain readers in their pay, who sit in the place of common resort, and read all the most interesting parts of the newspaper aloud—not unfrequently illustrating the subject with geographical and other notes, or by going back and referring to previous circumstances, of which the conclusion only happens to be detailed in the paper of the day.

The educative function, for good or ill, of the 'pothouse oracle' must have been important in creating political consciousness among his hearers.[71]

The working class reading public was certainly no single whole. Many of them, even if able to read a little, did no reading at all, beyond normal daily encounters with handbills or advertising. Others read only newspapers; still others read only to escape. As in any class at any time the number of students and eager or even moderately deep thinkers was very small. And, if this public was to be addressed on behalf of one or another social or political idea, a single approach would hardly serve. One did not talk to William Lovett and a coster in the same way. These groups were not impenetrable; some very significant ideas took a deep hold in the minds of those far removed from the little aristocracy of labour who, intellectually, could put most of the upper classes to shame. More advanced thinkers were certain that even the apathetic or hostile members of the working classes could be made amenable to reason, if reason could once be got inside their defences. It is the aim of this study to examine—of necessity incompletely —some of the important attempts to reason with, to indoctrinate that over-simplified abstraction, the working man, on a number of crucial subjects, related to the social and political problems of a threatening half century. The insights were few, the errors many. Both errors and insights are important. For this was a pioneering effort to solve the problem of getting ideas across from one man, or one class, to another. It is not a dead question.

CHAPTER II

THE REALIZATION OF THE PROBLEM

1790–1820

THE rapidly expanding output of political pamphlets and handbills played an important part in the widening political interests of the eighteenth century.[1] But in the nineties one finds a persistent overtone of novelty. The strangeness lay not so much in the variety and extent of publication as in a new complexity in the audience. For the first time the working class reader had specifically to be reckoned with.

Of the London radical groups, the two most active were the Society for Constitutional Information and the London Corresponding Society. The former, composed of educated and respectable gentlemen, was founded in 1780 by Major Cartwright and revived in the nineties to agitate for reform. The Corresponding Society drew on a lower level of society, the small but distinct aristocracy of artisans and mechanics. As one important part of its activity, it undertook to link together radical activity throughout the country. It also performed an educational function of the greatest importance. In 1794 Francis Place, then a poor journeyman tailor, joined a division in Covent Garden and later became a delegate to the General Committee. Years afterwards he wrote:

In this society I met with many inquisitive clever upright men and among them I greatly inlarged [sic] my acquaintance. They were in most if not in all respects superior to any with whom I had hitherto been acquainted. We had book subscriptions, similar to the breeches clubs, before mentioned, only the books for which any one subscribed were read by all the members in rotation who chose to read them before they were finally consigned to the subscriber. We had Sunday evening parties at the residence of those who could accommodate a number of persons. At these meetings we had readings, conversations, and discussions. There was [sic] at this time a great many such parties, they were highly useful and agreeable. The usual mode of proceeding at these weekly meetings was this. The chairman (each man was chairman in rotation), read from some book a chapter or part of a chapter, which as many as could read the chapter at their homes, the book passing from one to the other, had done, and at the next meeting a portion of the chapter was again read and the persons present were invited to make remarks thereon; as many as chose did so, but without rising. Then another portion was read and a second invitation was given—then the remainder was read and a third invitation was given when they who had not before spoken were expected to say something. Then there was a general discussion. No one was permitted to speak more than once during the reading. The same rule was observed in the general discussions, no one could speak a second time until every one who chose had spoken once, then any one might speak again, and so on till the subject was exhausted. . . .[2]

Provincial societies too illustrate a new orientation in political life. In turning over the pages of the *State Trials*, one is struck with the number of cordwainers, butchers, cutlers, and other artisans who were called as witnesses, and who admitted membership in radical organizations. Birmingham, Manchester, Leeds, and other industrial towns were centres of radical activity. In Norwich, the Revolution Society required members to contribute to the purchase of books. In Sheffield, a society of two thousand 'well-behaved men, most of them of the lower sort of workmen,' met regularly to discuss various subjects, especially government, and actively circulated literature and a local radical paper called *The Patriot*.[3]

The membership of these societies was exaggerated by supporters and opponents alike. Nor was their financial position encouraging. The L.C.S. asked only a penny a week from its members, and its journal for 16 May, 1793, shows quarterly receipts of some thirty pounds, and expenditures in printing, advertising, and incidentals of a little over twenty-three pounds. By the end of 1794—when repression had done much of its work—the Sheffield group had seriously curtailed their publishing, and in the next year, unable to pay for a room, had to resort to the open air.[4] Even with voluntary contributions to support a publishing programme, the threat to the peace seems hardly formidable. Yet the societies were active and feared. Fortunately it is not necessary here to go into the difficult question of how far the panic was justified. So far as the working class reader is concerned, the important factors are the nature of radical literature and its distribution.

Pride of place must go to Thomas Paine, and, of his writings, to the *Rights of Man*, the first part of which, in answer to Burke's *Reflections*, appeared in March, 1791. By the time the second part appeared in the next year, fifty thousand copies had been sold; and in 1793 the sale was estimated at two hundred thousand copies.[5] So large a sale was made possible by the low price at which later editions were sold, for many applications had come to the author for cheap editions or for permission to reprint. The Manchester Constitutional Society asked a local radical leader, Thomas Cooper, to abridge the work, so that it might be priced under a shilling.[6] Perhaps the best summing up of its impact is a revealing statement by Aikin, an annalist of the period. The cheap edition, he wrote, had enabled the work to circulate widely, 'and its success in making proselytes would have been a truly formidable circumstance, had their rank in society borne a proportion to their numbers.'[7]

Paine's other writings, too, were actively circulated. A plan of the Constitutional Society for the distribution of his *Letter to Mr. Secretary Dundas* indicates that twelve thousand copies were printed at a cost of twenty-five pounds; the nearly nine thousand copies accounted for by the plan were to go to thirty-six individuals or societies, usually one to two hundred to each, while twelve hundred each went to correspondents in Manchester, Norwich, and Sheffield. A letter from the secretary of the London Corresponding Society acknowledges receipt of two hundred copies of the *Letter* and four hundred copies of other publications. With careful distribution, he said, 'those 600 papers shall be seen by as many thousand persons.'[8]

To get an accurate picture of the publishing activities of the societies is difficult. In the first place, they usually resolved to print very large numbers—one hundred thousand is not uncommon; surely many proposed publications never appeared, and quantities must rarely have exceeded a few thousand. Secondly, the methods of financing are not at all clear. The costs of printing and advertising—a common method of getting radical propaganda to the public—were far from negligible. Publications for free distribution were limited by small budgets, so that other propaganda had to be either sold or subsidized by voluntary donations.[9] But the astonishing variety of material which has survived, despite the ephemeral nature of such publications, seems to indicate that the activity was on a large scale. Most of them were sold, and, judging from the chapbook trade, such publication was probably largely self-supporting.

While some of the literature was surely too rationalistic or remote to appeal to any but the dedicated, the many lively local productions must certainly have been attractive even to casual readers. *Rights of Swine: An Address to the Poor*, printed at Stockport in 1794, is heavy with the economic crisis.[10] A halfpenny broadside in the form of a last dying speech of Tom Paine was published in Birmingham, an ironic radical comment on Paine's being burned in effigy there in 1793. Another Birmingham production was Kit Morris's *Political Glossary* of 1795, in which 'envy and admiration of the world' is defined as 'Pitt and Co's valuable and numerous places and pensions,' and 'Father of his People' as 'The —— Farmer cramming the empty stomachs of the poor with ——' From Manchester came *A Rod for the Burkites . . . by One of the 'Swinish Multitude'*. Ballads were popular forms, and a 1793 Edinburgh collection of songs was pointedly called *Twopence Worth of Hogs Bristles, for the Use of the Rabble*. Ridgway in London published a radical tale called *The Village Association, or the Politics of Edley*. And in a penny publication of 1795 called *Church and King Morality* is a long list of the publications of T. G. Ballard, 'bookseller to . . . the Swine of Westminster,' which range from the works of Paine and Thelwall, to an 'Impartial Address to All Parties by a Lady' at threepence, 'No Placemen, No Pensioners, or the System of Corruption Unmasked' and ' Tax and Axe' at twopence, 'License for the Guinea Pigs to Wear Powder' and a great variety of songs and pasquinades at a penny. The idiom seems little different from that of present-day publications by political parties out of power.

Clearly the threatening element from the government point of view was the extension of political agitation to segments of society hitherto relatively untouched. Windham referred in the House to 'alarming discontents actively propagated by seditious publications,' and Pitt called for 'a great deal of activity on the part of the friends of our constitution, to take pains properly to address the public mind, and to keep it in that state which was necessary to our present tranquillity.' Even in late 1795, Sir John Scott, the future Lord Eldon, was still lamenting the prevalence of libels, so numerous as to defeat all attempts at wholesale prosecution under present law.[11]

As the price fell, the liability of radical publications to prosecution became greater. The attorney-general stated that he did not prosecute the first part of the *Rights of Man* because, reprehensible though it was, the circumstances of its publication would confine it to the judicious reader who could refute it as he went along. But, when the second part appeared, and when 'in all shapes, in all sizes, with an industry incredible, it was either totally or partially thrust into the hands of all persons in this country, of subjects of every description; when . . . even children's sweetmeats were wrapped up with parts of this . . .,' he had no choice but to prosecute. Sir John Scott told Thomas Cooper that he might publish his *Reply to Burke's Invective* freely in octavo form, but as soon as it was published cheaply, a libel action would be taken. And the Recorder of London, before whom Daniel Isaac Eaton was on trial for a seditious libel allegedly contained in his lively publication, *Hog's Wash*, declared that, while the libel must be decided on other grounds, the cheapness of the paper, if it were found to be a libel, would aggravate the offence.[12]

Repressive measures taken as a result of the panic among the upper classes were sweeping, harsh, and effective. Prosecution of individuals reached its climax in the heavy sentences of transportation laid on the leaders of the Edinburgh Convention. Habeas corpus was suspended in 1794, and acts of the following year limited the holding of public meetings and extended the scope of high treason. The radical societies began to disappear, with a final blow dealt by the Corresponding Societies Act of 1799, which also imposed strict control by justices of the peace on the printing trade.

The government's action against seditious publications was effective too, despite Scott's fulminations. On 21 May, 1792, a royal proclamation was issued against seditious writings, which Richard Carlile, the radical publisher, believed seriously interfered with the sale of the *Rights of Man*. A Sheffield plater testified that its condemnation as a libel in 1792 stopped its circulation by the radical society there. A bill-sticker appointed by the L.C.S. to post the 'Answer to the Place and Pension Club' was hauled off to Bow Street and committed to Tothill Fields for six months.[13] There were indirect means, too, of getting at seditious literature. Letters from the L.C.S. to Norwich and Birmingham correspondents refer to the possibility of interception in the post; and publicans were threatened with the loss of their licenses, if they permitted political conversations or provided seditious prints.[14]

Suppression was not, however, the only string to the government's bow. Even before the end of 1791 a counter-attack had started. Paine noted that several answers had been written against his book, but he took comfort in the belief that they 'did not excite reading enough to pay the expense of the printing.'[15] Twenty-two thousand copies of an undoubtedly scurrilous pamphlet called *Strictures on Thomas Paine's Works and Character* were printed in Portsmouth in 1792-3, on a subsidy from the secret service fund.[16] George Chalmers's *Life of Pain* [sic] went through several editions. The second, in cheap form, carries a note: 'Read this, and then hand it to others who are requested to do likewise.' This is probably the life of Paine which the Bishop of London recommended to Hannah More. 'It is curious, entertaining, and authentic. That life and the pamphlet (which I enclose to you under another cover) are the best antidotes I have seen to the poison of his publications; they ought to be printed in cheap penny pamphlets, and dispersed over the kingdom.'[17] The abridged edition in the British Museum published in 1793, containing twenty-six pages and sold at a shilling or two guineas per hundred, clearly to expedite free distribution, also contains advertisements for fifteen other publications for cheap circulation, some priced as low as a penny, or two guineas per thousand. Perhaps the most celebrated of the anti-reform tracts was *Village Politics, Addressed to All the Mechanics, Journeymen, and Labourers, in Great Britain, by Will Chip, a Country Carpenter,* written anonymously by Hannah More, whose *Cheap Repository Tracts* have already been mentioned. Her most recent biographer has described it as 'Burke for Beginners.'[18] In form it is typical: a dialogue in which the solid blacksmith inevitably wins the argument over the silly radical mason. How often in such publications the victor is identified with the rural complex —he is frequently a farm labourer—while the vanquished is an artisan or small shopkeeper! The laboured humour, the contrived heartiness, the identification of dissipation and radicalism, and the notion of leaving politics to one's betters are common to the species. So is the clear use of upper class distribution. The author's identity did not remain a secret, and the tract was received with great enthusiasm. The Bishop of London assured Miss More that it was 'universally extolled,' that it was admired at Windsor, and that the attorney-general had recommended it to the Association at the Crown and Anchor, of which more presently. Her friend, Mrs. Montagu, called it 'the most generally approved and universally useful of any thing that has been published in the present exigency of the times,' sent copies to all her correspondents, and announced that the parson of her Northumberland parish intended to get a thousand copies. The government apparently sent copies to Scotland and Ireland in quantity, while wealthy individuals printed editions for circulation at their own expense.[19] And the strength of its reputation is indicated by its survival to be re-issued during the unrest of the post-war period and the crises of the early thirties.

Of much greater importance, as a symptom of the panic and as a publishing venture, is the activity of the Association for Preserving Liberty and Property against Republicans and Levellers, more commonly known as the 'Crown and Anchor' or the 'Loyal Association,' founded in 1792. The leading spirit was John Reeves, barrister and legal writer, who maintained close connexions with the *Anti-Jacobin* group. The 'principal citizens' of London met at the Crown and Anchor on 20

November, 1792, and formed an association to discourage and suppress seditious publications, to support the laws protecting persons and property, and 'occasionally to explain those topics of public discussion, which have been so perverted by evil designing men, and to shew, by irrefragable proofs, that they are not applicable to the state of this country, that they can produce no good, and certainly must produce much evil.' To accomplish these aims, it was recommended that all friends of order establish similar societies in other areas. It was said that within the next year two thousand or more such groups were formed throughout the kingdom. Radical opponents alleged that the associations were government supported, but this was denied by the Association in London.[20]

Subscriptions in London were apparently heavy, for a most remarkable publishing programme was undertaken at once. One part consisted largely of ordinary pamphlet material, charges to grand juries, speeches, and sermons, including the *Short Hints upon Levelling* by William Vincent, later Dean of Westminster, and Paley's *Reasons for Contentment, Addressed to the Labouring Part of the British Public*. A second group was chosen by an editor to aim primarily at the lower classes—an aim which, the committee hastened to add by way of absolution, accounted for the style and manner and the inclusion of ballad at the end of each pamphlet, to assure that something was provided for every taste. This group contained forty tracts, among them Hannah More's *Village Politics*, an analysis of the *Rights of Man*, some atrocity stories about the French, *One Pennyworth of Truth from Thomas Bull to His Brother John, Think a Little, The Englishman's Political Catechism*, and *Poor Richard, or, The Way to Wealth and Content in These Troublous Times*. For sheer size, the performance is astounding. The separate items were published not only as pamphlets, but as broadsides and handbills, some of which are still to be seen in the British Museum. Walls were plastered with them, and alehouses were provided with them, while similar and smaller societies over the country distributed these tracts and printed their own. The supporters of the status quo were worried indeed.[21]

Provincial activity was great, but space can be spared only for one large-scale effort, which began with some letters to Dr. Priestley in 1790, published under the pseudonym of

'John Nott,' allegedly one John Morfitt. A reply of the same year is called *Very Familiar Letters Addressed to Mr. John Nott, Button-Burnisher . . . by Alexander Armstrong, Whip-maker, and Abel Sharp, Spur-maker*; both tracts are largely religious controversy. In 1792 Old Job Nott came into the field with his anti-radical *Humble Advice*, which appeared both as pamphlet and broadside and went through at least five editions. His subsequent *Life and Adventures* went through at least twelve. A reformist reply, *An Appeal to the Inhabitants of Birmingham*, was directed against Job Nott by John Nott, his elder brother, a button-maker, and 'first cousin to John Nott, button-burnisher.' The food riots of 1795 produced *A Word to the Wise: or John Nott's . . . Opinion of the Riot in Snow-Hill* at a penny for eight octavo pages, 'with large Allowance to those who buy to sell again.'

The author of the Job Nott pamphlets is generally believed to have been Theodore Price, of Harborne, a merchant at Kingston Wharf, Cambridge Street, although the Rev. R. Burn is sometimes given credit for assistance. Price, justice of the peace and obviously a dedicated man, was blessed with a pungent style and was successful enough to be flattered by imitation. After a rash of pamphlets during the wars, the Nott family retired, until the *Searcher* was published in 1817; and in the crisis of 1819 the whole flock appeared—Job Nott, jun., John Nott, jun., Tobias, William, Jeremiah (printed in London), Jemimah, and Richard. Other Nott publications appear, from various publishers, in 1827-28, 1832, 1835-37, and, finally, *Job Nott's Twelve Affectionate Addresses*, from 1847 to 1852, again largely religious controversy. The later productions are much inferior to those of the 1790's and 1819; the only subsequent writer really to catch the Nott style was the man responsible for the *Bristol Job Nott*, an anti-radical weekly published from 1831 to 1833.[22]

Except for a burst of pamphlets during the invasion panic of 1803-4,[23] the first decade of the nineteenth century saw little activity of the sort discussed here. Repression had done its work, and apparently the radical threat had passed. The attempts of the nineties to counteract radical propaganda are of course far from exhausted by this brief and selective sketch; but it has been made clear that the upper classes were deeply conscious of a new sort of threat which could not be met alone by reading the Riot Act or calling out a company of soldiers. The efforts of both individuals and societies were almost entirely defensive and *ad hoc*. A general inculcation of quietism and religious principles aside, there was little trace of an upper class offensive on positive lines,[24] a failure which can perhaps be best accounted for by the novelty of the problem and by the great gulf which separated 'the poor' from their superiors.

The great majority of the working classes were at this time still 'church and king'; the rioting of the nineties found different objects than the rioting of twenty years later. So, for much of the population, the little publications and the grubbing about among chapmen and their wares to learn the technique of popular literature had perhaps little necessity, though it may well have found some response. At any rate, Place wrote years later that the Loyal Association's tracts and songs, 'such as a sweep would now be ashamed of,' were distributed by the toll takers at turnpike gates, 'and they made every silly soul outrageously loyal.'[25] But the loyalists failed to discern the real portent: that the active radicals were those rapidly disengaging themselves from the strata below—men who could not be captured by garish woodcuts or converted by the preaching of rural virtues. Among these small groups of self-educated, devoted, and class-conscious men were to be found the leaders of working class movements, when the lower classes, exasperated by the failure of their betters to solve, or often even to notice, the terrible complications of industrial and agrarian change, became in good part radical almost overnight.

*

The Luddite troubles of 1811-13 were largely spontaneous and unorganized, but no upheaval can take place without its printers. Handbills and posters there had to be, if only to advertise meetings for reform.[26] But a writer in the *Quarterly Review* saw more than that; he complained of 'anarchist journalists' who dominated the weekly and infiltrated the daily press, 'inflaming the turbulent temper of the manufacturer, and disturbing the quiet attachment of the peasant to those institutions under which he and his fathers have dwelt in peace.' There are references to inflammatory handbills and seditious papers in correspondence with the Home Office, and the prosecution in one of the York trials in 1813 announced that an accomplice would reveal that the accused had worked in a shop where it was a practice to read accounts of the machine-breaking at Nottingham.[27] There are also indications that the press was used for a certain amount of counter-propaganda in Manchester.[28]

These instances to the contrary, it seems probable that the press was of relatively little importance at this time. Occasional productions like those of the nineties were certainly inhibited by the war. Newspapers were still expensive and hard to come by.[29] The greatest of radical journalists was in gaol in 1812 and had not yet discovered where his real strength lay. The records of trials for the most part are as silent regarding the press as modern students of the period. And the alarmist reports of committees of Parliament on the threat to public order, which one would expect to exploit every available item, germane to the issue or not, make only one reference to 'inflammatory placards.'[30]

How different is the case with the 1817 reports![31] If in 1812 the green bags held no serious evidence of radical printing, in 1817 they most assuredly did. The secret committee of the Commons cited the propagation of subversive doctrines by speakers, while 'they have been circulated with incredible activity and perseverance, in cheap and often gratuitous publications.' Moreover, the societies charged a small subscription each week which went to pay the 'missionaries' and to purchase seditious tracts which were read and discussed at their meetings. The Lords' committee referred to the 'unremitting activity . . . in circulating to an unprecedented extent, at the lowest prices or gratuitously, publications of the most seditious and inflammatory nature. . . .'

Debates in Parliament abound in examples of concern. Lord Sidmouth in 1817 assured the Lords that the industry with which sedition was spread had never before been matched, and in 1819 he announced that seditious publications were to be found 'in every cottage in some districts of the kingdom (he thanked God not in all).' Lord Liverpool maintained that the dangers of 1817 far outstripped those of 1794, while the present conspirators, having profited by the example of the former, proceeded with greater caution and management. And the attorney-general echoed Sir John Scott in lamenting the profusion and cleverness of the libels which made effective prosecution impossible.[32] The Whigs talked down the menace to some extent, but disowned sedition. Brougham held that nothing could be more injurious to society than what had been put out in the twopenny pamphlets, and he charged the ministers with neglect in not having attempted 'to stop that torrent of blasphemy and sedition which had lately inundated the country, before it had arrived at its present height. The existing laws conferred on them sufficient power wherewith to have done it.'[33]

To alarmists in the country the Whigs were simply blind. A critic of Lord Fitzwilliam's attack on the Peterloo magistrates insisted that the press was teaching rebellion, assassination, and violent revolution, and demonstrated the tendency by pointing to advertisements of the works of Voltaire and Mirabaud which were 'in preparation for *popular perusal*—to be issued from our revolutionary presses, in *very cheap editions* —and these editions *in numbers*—for more easy and general circulation among the populace.' And another pamphleteer noted that loyalty and religion where not only exploded but laughed at. 'Dustmen and porters read and discuss politics; and labourers, journeymen, and masters speak *one language of disaffection and defiance.*'[34]

Precisely what was the seditious press? Richard Carlile is an instructive example. He came to London as a tinplate journeyman, threw himself into politics, and began to write.

In 1817 the *Black Dwarf* made its appearance, which happened to be much more to my taste than Mr. Cobbett's *Registers*. Having purchased the first two numbers, and lent them to as many of my fellow-workmen as would read them and got illegibly black, [sic] I wrote a letter and enclosed them to George Canning, and requested him, after he had read them, to hand them over to Castlereagh for the Green Bag that was then on the table of the House of Commons, particularly pointing out to him how well they had been read, as was evident from their appearance.[35]

Carlile began to distribute Wooler's paper regularly and sold other publications, one of which he made eventually into the *Republican*. T. J. Wooler, under whom Carlile served his apprenticeship, was a Yorkshire printer transplanted to London. His *Black Dwarf* began to appear in 1817, an eight-page quarto weekly at fourpence; in 1820 it became a thirty-six page octavo publication at sixpence. This is a high price, but the *Dwarf* was exceedingly popular throughout the country, and, for some reason, especially among the miners of the Northeast. When Cobbett fled the country in 1817, sales of the *Register* fell sharply, and Wooler's paper replaced it as the chief radical unstamped journal. Its sale was reported as 12,000 weekly. The Place set now in the British Museum contains also a number of posters advertising issues of the paper, certain to attract attention by the blackness of the letters, and likely to introduce some questions into the reader's mind, even if he were not to read the journal itself. In 1818 Wooler also published Bentham's *Catechism of Parliamentary Reform*, 'with the style adapted to the popular reader,' in ten fourpenny numbers.[36] Wade's *Gorgon* was helped on by contributions from Bentham and Place. There were other London papers—*Medusa*, *Cap of Liberty*, the *Briton*, the *White Hat*. Provincial radical papers had begun to appear.[37] And special mention should be given to William Hone, an old radical, who formed a fruitful partnership with Cruikshank; their best-known product was *The Political House that Jack Built*, which attained an immense popularity—great enough to call out answers in the same style.[38] Hone also gained a considerable amount of abuse for his parodies of the Catechism, Creed, and Litany.

The provinces were in ferment. The Leicester Hampden Club, when it was organized towards the end of 1816, decided to purchase a hundred copies weekly of Cobbett's *Register* to sell at twopence each to further the cause. In Manchester, an observer commented on the state of feeling in public houses where the talk was all irreverent and revolutionary, and where the 'oracles [were] the *Statesman* newspaper, *Independent Whig* and *Cobbett's Register*.' And to this must be added the influence of the local radical paper, the *Observer*.[39] Every important town had its radical publisher and bookseller, like John Marshall in Newcastle or Sutton and Son in Nottingham. Birmingham was active not only with pamphlets and broadsides, but with weekly papers, like the *Inspector* and George Edmonds' *Weekly Recorder* and *Register*. The London papers circulated throughout the country. In November, 1819, Thomas Hodgskin wrote to Place from Edinburgh:

> You may perhaps judge of the manner in which things go on here in some measure when I tell you that an advertisement appeared here a few days ago telling the people as a sort of phenomena [sic] that the Black Dwarf—Cobbet [sic] and the Republican were to be procured by application at a particular miserable room in one of the miserable *Closes* of this city in which they were sold—I should say but for the advertisement, by stealth. None however were at the moment to be procured, the last ship load being exhausted. One of those twopenny papers which have been so useful in the neighbourhood of London has recently been published here under the name of the Patriot and like all the rest is strong for liberty. It is the only publication here in which the prosecution of Carlisle [sic] was condemned as intolerant. It is however very low and vulgar. I mean that there is a mixture of indecency and puerility. It is however good to see something of the kind.

He reported at the end of the month that the seller of these papers had been apprehended and was to be tried.[40]

Undoubtedly the most important radical publisher was William Cobbett. Egotistic, quarrelsome, inconsistent, and really tory, he was the best writer in the business, and to the frightened upper classes, like Paine before him, he was the incarnation of the devil. His change from anti-jacobin activity to radicalism was slow in maturing. By 1807 he was already active in the radical politics of Westminster, and the riots of 1811 and 1812—and his stay in gaol—drew his attention to industrial areas and brought their workers into his calculations beside his agricultural labourers and London artisans. In 1816 he was ready with his plan.[41] His paper, the *Political Register*, had been issued at 1s. o½d., and groups of workmen had clubbed together to buy it. Now, learning that publicans were threatened with loss of licenses and that government papers were advocating cheap propaganda, he decided to sell his paper at a price working men could afford—twopence, excluding news to avoid the tax. The success of the scheme was immediate. By the end of November, 1816, he could insert the triumphant notice that forty-four thousand copies of the first cheap number had been printed and sold. 'Let Corruption *rub that out*, if she can.' Bentham in 1817 spoke of the circulation of the paper as sixty thousand, which may be something of an exaggeration; but forty to fifty thousand is certain, and that figure must be multiplied by perhaps ten to ascertain roughly the numbers of readers.[42] Colonel Fletcher of Bolton wrote to the Home Office that 'there is scarcely a street or a post in the Land but that is placarded with something seditious,' and he included a letter from a spy which said: 'Cobatt [sic] hath done more with his Twopenny papers than any Thousand beside him, as any one can get them, the price being so low and Contains so much matter as the Children purchase and Read them.' It was read regularly at club meetings; and Samuel Bamford, by supplying it to some sergeants in a canteen, went at least some way to justify Southey's fears that such 'manifestoes as those of Cobbett, Hone, and the *Examiner*,' found in ale-houses where troops were quartered, would seduce soldiers from their duty.[43]

Cobbett's radicalism was that of Major Cartwright with his own twists. His *bete-noire* was finance—the sinking fund, pensions, sinecures, salaries, the 'Pitt system,' taxation. His cure was parliamentary reform and annual parliaments. Again and again he emphasized that he wanted no innovations, but only what Englishmen had once had. But his reassuring statements would hardly be noticed by the upper classes who read more violent things that he said. Middle class radicals were not happy about him, for he rejected their leadership and hated their political economy, making, said the *Westminster Review*, 'fundamental mistakes which deprived him of his authority except among the less instructed. What he addressed most successfully, were the prejudices and passions of men; their pride, vanity, selfishness, and hatred.'[44]

His hold on his audience was most impressive. Opponents taunted him with inconsistency, especially with that between the anti-jacobin *Register* and the radical *Register*—hardly a wise choice of ground, for Cobbett had openly recanted. His lesser inconsistencies did get some attention, and the *Poor Man's Guardian*, which caused more horror than Cobbett in the thirties, certainly pointed them out; yet its editors recognized that his eccentricities were privileged, that he had 'established for himself a sort of prescriptive right to be inconsistent on all manner of subjects, without, at the same time, destroying his influence as an able and most useful political writer.'[45] How much greater must have been the confidence of less reflective persons!

The secret of his appeal is two-fold, and it is important to understand it, to provide a standard for judging other writers for the working classes. First, there is his style. Even his enemies realized that. They saw, and wished they could imitate, his vigour, simplicity, and raciness. They objected to his coarseness and vituperation which our less respectable generation can appreciate as Cobbett's readers must have done. They objected too that he had no invention, no imagination, no capacity to generalize or to state broad principles. But not only did these critics misread the Cobbett of the *Rural Rides*; they also, as usual, misread his audience, for whom only a direct, simple, completely concrete approach could have any meaning. Better than any other public man, wrote John Doherty, the union leader, Cobbett understood the character and interests of his countrymen, and the working of the wicked system that had brought the country to its dire position.[46] And precisely as he was earthbound, he was able to make that system, as he saw it, plain to the simple, materially concerned people for whom he wrote. The second and perhaps more important quality of Cobbett's writing and personality is closely related. The *Athenaeum* saw it and drew the conclusion which no one, or almost no one, among the upper classes was able to follow. If those who railed at his works would read them, they would find that

> Mr. Cobbett's personal consciousness of all which is concealed from our eyes by grey jackets and clouted shoes, has kept alive his sympathy with the majority of mankind; and this is indeed a merit, which can be attributed to but few political writers.[47]

Such were the men who wrote and published the radical papers and pamphlets. Most of them were able, daring, and devoted. That they found the business undoubtedly profitable[48] does not detract from their reputation, as their enemies hoped it might do when they made wild charges of profiteering on the pennies of deluded readers. Indeed, it indicates how well they did their job; and had they looked out only for profits, Cobbett would surely not have fled the country, nor would Carlile have gone so often to prison, as did many other editors and publishers of the 'unstamped' in the thirties. But devotion was not the monopoly of the publishers; there were also the large numbers of usually forgotten people who sold and distributed the papers. They too made a profit—Cobbett said that the income from a sale of three or four hundred *Registers* per week would support a small family, and cited one man who had cleared three pounds fifteen shillings by selling 1,800 papers—but they ran serious risks as well. Sellers were often arrested and detained, and a clerical J.P. wrote to the Home Secretary in 1817 that he had had 'two men . . . apprehended for distributing Cobbett's Pamphlets, and had them well flogged at the whipping post.'[49] The cause of the 'unstamped,' of freedom of the press, was not without its martyrs. And, so long as there was discontent and political excitement, there was an audience, a large one and working class.

Clearly something had to be done. In 1817 Sidmouth sent his famous Circular Letter to the Lords-lieutenant, advising them of an opinion of the law officers that any justice of the peace might issue a warrant to take a person charged with libel and to demand bail for his release.[50] The suspension of habeas corpus in the same year was aimed in part at controlling the press, and two of the Six Acts of 1819 were concerned with 'twopenny trash.' But legal action, prosecution, and informers make up a story which has been told elsewhere. What was done to carry out the challenge in Sidmouth's statement at the end of 1818 that Cobbett 'must be written down?' Immediately, said the proposed victim, a host of little pamphlets sprang up about the country, while several appeared in London, ' one of which could not cost less than *two thousand guineas* in advertising in large and expensive *placards*, which were pulled down, or effaced, the hour they were put up, and which were replaced the next hour, as one wave succeeds another in the sea.'

The effort which Cobbett singled out for special attack was called *Anti-Cobbett*, 'published at the same identical office which George Rose originally set up with the public money,' and written by Canning, Gifford, and Southey. The expenses of publication and advertising, he thought, must have reached twenty thousand pounds before he left England.[51] The masthead of the paper is similar to that of the *Register*; the price was rather pointedly set at three halfpence. It ran from 15 February to 5 April, 1817, eight numbers in all; and the address in the last number perhaps best indicates its purpose and method:

> This publication . . . has convicted [Cobbett] out of his own mouth. It has opened the eyes of many thousands, in all parts of the kingdom, who could not believe it possible that a man should be so utterly shameless, and destitute of all principle, as Cobbett has here been shewn to be, not by garbled extracts from his various writings, but by long compositions, such as Cobbett's Life of Paine, Cobbett's Instructive Essay on the French Revolution, and Cobbett's Bloody Buoy; not to mention the numerous shorter passages, all in the same strain, from his various publications for twelve years together.

Each issue contained sixteen pages, usually an address, a song or two, and perhaps one of the extracts from Cobbett. The first issue, for example, included a doggerel poem contrasting the old and new meanings of 'Reformers' and 'Patriots,' and an open letter devoted to Cobbett's inconsistency and poking fun at his historically indefensible statements about the guarantees of Magna Carta. The second exposed him as 'the very hinge of a great plan of Insurrection and Massacre,' and summarized the report of the Commons' secret committee.

Publishers, organizations, and government were all active in the campaign against Cobbett. Blackwood, in Edinburgh, published *The Political Death of Mr. William Cobbett* in 1820, bringing early Cobbett to bear on later Cobbett. Selected passages from early *Registers* also made up the *Politics for the People by William Cobbett*, published at a penny by the Birmingham Association for the Refutation and Suppression of Blasphemy and Sedition; while their *Letter to William Cobbett* pointed out his 'hypocrisy and apostasy' regarding Paine, whose bones he had brought back from America, but whom he had once execrated.[52] But a writer in a Glasgow paper denounced these attempts to smear the reputation of a writer whose enemies dared not face him in fair argument. Cobbett, he pointed out, had recanted his early positions; but, even allowing him to be inconsistent, how could sixpenny worth of such stuff as the anti-Cobbett pamphlets satisfy hunger or obliterate Peterloo?[53]

Wooler too came in for counter-attack. The writer of a Newcastle pamphlet in 1819 was almost beside himself over the skill and depravity of the *Black Dwarf* and the degradation of its audience, who, having nothing to lose, preferred demolition to preservation.[54] But the best known of the opposition papers is the *White Dwarf*, edited by Gibbons Merle on a subsidy from the Home Secretary. For some reason the payment was stopped, and the paper came to an end with the twenty-second number in April, 1818. There were recriminations in which Merle threatened to publish his confidential correspondence with the Home Office, and he promised a future paper with some interesting disclosures about important people, but the threats were never carried out.

Like Wooler's paper, the *White Dwarf* consisted of sixteen pages and sold at fourpence, a price Merle refused to reduce. In general, the style is inflated, the sentences and words are long, and the question arises—as it does so often in these publications—of precisely what audience was intended. The general nature of the comments and the tone hardly seem adapted to the working classes, although the prospectus indicated 'a general intention to undeceive you respecting certain publications and certain persons, by whose insinuations, errors, and industry united, you are in danger of being betrayed.' The second number, 6 December, 1817, contains an address to the labouring classes, assuring them of the good intentions of the editors, however unpalatable may be the truths put forward, and urging them to club together to buy the paper. But this address is preceded by another to 'manufacturers, land holders, and others,' in which they are assigned a missionary role—'warm and philanthropic exertions on your side' being the only hope of success with minds so fearfully inflamed.

On the whole, however, Merle seems to have been concerned primarily with the lower middle classes and the upper ranks of artisans. In the issue of 28 February, 1818, he makes a clear distinction between the *populace* and the *people*. The former were apparently written off as hopelessly lost and not worth saving; the task lay with the latter whom he defines as traders, shopkeepers, clerks, and mechanics, who would suffer intensely by the devastation proposed by the agitators. They were tainted as well.

Meanwhile, up in Islington, another instructive experiment was proceeding. W. H. Shadgett, a petty clerk, apparently seeing an opportunity for bettering his position in joining the presumably wealthy ranks of the anti-radicals, began to publish *Shadgett's Weekly Review of Cobbett, Wooler, Sherwin, and Other Democratical and Infidel Writers*, 'designed as an antidote to their dangerous and destructive doctrines, and to desseminate [sic] just and sound principles, on all popular subjects.' It ran to seventy-eight numbers, from the first of February, 1818 to 26 July, 1819. An eight-page sheet, it was published every Sunday, an anti-sabbatical act immediately questioned and explained as advisable to counteract the great majority of Sunday papers which were subversive, and to assure its presence on a day of leisure. The price was fourpence. Cobbett's, Wooler's, and Sherwin's papers were regularly reviewed; Hone, Wade, Paine, and Voltaire came in for attention; and there were ordinary anti-reform and religious articles.

Clearly the editor's hopes were not realized. In June, 1818, an address mentioned both public approbation and lack of capital. Establishing the paper cost two hundred pounds, and a subsequent debt nearly equalled that figure; current loss was five pounds a week. Shadgett was imprisoned for debt, and a committee of his supporters was formed to examine his affairs and to raise a subscription, but the sum received fell just short of fifty-four pounds. By January, 1819, Shadgett was complaining of the lukewarmness of booksellers and newsagents, and in the middle of the year he threw up the publication and went to Quebec.[55]

Space cannot be spared for more than a few suggestions of the extent of anti-radical publishing in London and the provinces; even to list all the pamphlets, dialogues, tales, and addresses in various local collections is impossible in a chapter which makes no pretence at being either exhaustive or definitive.

In 1819 the Society for Promoting Christian Knowledge set up a committee to expedite the distribution of anti-infidel tracts. These tracts were, of course, almost entirely religious, but the minutes of the Committee are useful in throwing some light on problems of distribution. In December, 1819, the Bishop of Chester urged that tracts should be bound up in small volumes, 'as there is an obvious danger of single sheet, and other small Tracts being lost, or destroyed by People of the lower Classes. . . .' In January, 1820, a sub-committee of correspondence reported that in Manchester great difficulty was encountered in getting the poor to take the tracts, even on personal application from those to whom they were most obliged, and that the hawkers were uniformly unfriendly. Reports from Bolton were equally discouraging. By April over a hundred booksellers in London had been appointed agents; considerable numbers of tracts were sold in the West End, but in the eastern parts of the city, especially in the Borough, Spitalfields, Shoreditch, and Bethnal Green, it was hard to find tradesmen who would take them in, and the demand, 'as anticipated,' was trifling. The Bishop of Chester was of opinion that the disaffected were too poor to buy tracts and would not in any event, so the sub-committee determined to distribute large numbers free in about twenty of the most populous parishes of that diocese. By the end of November, 1820, about seven hundred thousand tracts had been issued to the public at an expense of four thousand pounds, or about half the fund available for the purpose. Prices were reduced; but, to judge from the information cited here, large numbers and firm financial backing could hardly have made up for the discouraging reception in important places.[56]

Hannah More, despite her seventy-five years, was once more into the breach. She wrote songs for *Anti-Cobbett*. *Village Politics* was refurbished for the new circumstances, and over a dozen new tracts came from her pen.[57] London publishers, like Hatchard and Seeley, turned out numbers of cheap anti-reform pamphlets. George Cayley, a physician, published two addresses to pitmen and keelmen at Durham in 1819; Edward Walker in Newcastle printed *A Word on the Other Side*, *The Friendly Fairy*, *The History of Thomas Whitehead*, and reprinted Paley's *Reasons for Contentment*. Sunderland printers produced some 'reflections' by Cobbett and reprinted Bowdler's famous *Reform or Ruin*, a call for political reformers to reform themselves.[58] In Edinburgh, Blackwood, as might be expected, was active; and a loyal society was set up to fight 'Disaffection with her own weapons '; but, despite the zeal and prominence of some individuals connected with it, its supporters became discouraged after publishing a few pamphlets and gave up the ghost. It is interesting to speculate on the cause of the failure, but no facts are forthcoming.[59]

The *Leeds Intelligencer* in 1819 published a penny *Reformers' Guide* and also issued a loyal paper called *The Domestic Miscellany; and Poor Man's Friend*, which sold at threepence for sixteen octavo pages of a somewhat slanted nature, and which ran for seven numbers. Manchester was a very active centre for loyalist printers. A periodical called *The Patriot* appeared after Peterloo; it sold for twopence and ran from 28 August to 1 January, 1820, when it fell victim, as did many of its opponents, to the new press laws. There were numbers of dialogues and similar productions. The Pitt Club in 1817 distributed two by Canon C. D. Wray, *The Speech of Mr. John P—, Schoolmaster . . .*, and *The Street Politicians*; and in the same year Francis Philips wrote *A Dialogue between Thomas, the Weaver, and His Old Master*.[60] Birmingham was similarly busy with reprints and new tracts, and the whole of the Nott tribe re-appeared with additions, particularly in a twopenny fortnightly periodical called *The Searcher*. Perhaps a sample should be given. In the issue of 10 March, 1817, Moses Nott added a postscript:

Just as I was sealing my letter, who should come in but cousin Betty Nott. She lives a little way out of town, and is in the washing line; but she's a desperate sharp wench, and can do what our good old King wished he might live to see *all* his subjects able to do; she can read the Bible, Mr. Editor, and what's more she lives up to it; she makes it the rule of her life. Nevertheless, she's a shrewd young hussy and can see as far as most; so I must tell you what she said to my letter. . . . 'Ah, Moses,' says she, 'but you stand no chance with old Cobb: *I've* read his books, and I tell you you stand no chance with him whatsomever. But, I think,' says she, 'I can put you in the way. You should come to our Sow and Pigs ale-house; there's Bill Wagstaff, the *cow-leech*, and Bob Pole-evil, the *dog horse-butcher*, and there's rough Sam, the *pig-driver*, and Joe Jazey, the *skull-thatcher*, four of the biggest blackguards in all our neighbourhood; *they're* your men for Old Cobb. . . . Put on your shabbiest clothes, and splash yourself all over with mud, and, for the vallee of a pint of ale, you'll hear all their slang; and *then*, and not *till* then, you'll be a match for Old Cobb.'

The Searcher was hardly a sincere attempt to convince working class radicals of the error of their ways. The passage quoted clearly reveals—for a respectable audience—hate, fear, and contempt. Two years later, Edmonds' radical paper was treating the Notts to attacks in their own scurrilous style.[61] By 1819 exasperation had carried all before it; writers were writing to partisans; and the real problems of the working class reader were lost in the battling.

In the post-war period as during the French Revolution, the attempt to meet the challenge of the working class reader was two-fold—effective repression and ineffective counter-propaganda. In trying to write down the radicals, the defenders of order and the status quo made no bold experiments, but held closely to the traditional means of moral and religious instruction, to tracts, dialogues, sermons, addresses, and so forth. As before, their efforts were *ad hoc* and defensive. Where reason was expected to have little effect, recourse was had to satire, jokes, invective, and scurrility. This was true of both sides, and the violence increased as the tension rose, reaching a climax after Peterloo and with the split in the country over the Queen's trial. Half amused, half sincere attempts to approximate the 'popular style' or to reproduce the slogans and catch-phrases which got a response from the less aware ebullience of the eighteenth century only indicated the extent of the separation between classes. Some writers realized that a superior order of workman had appeared—the *White Dwarf*, for example, was meant for the mechanics, artisans, shopkeepers, and petty clerks on the blurring borderline between the classes—and it was realized that they had been won over to radicalism. It was, however, not so easy to realize the extent of the radical victory, or the impact on intelligent and active minds of years of suffering and frustration and of a set of persuasive doctrines.

The radical press survived the Six Acts. Indeed, the political excitement of the Queen's trial in 1820 gave its writers one of their greatest opportunities. The repulsive and ludicrous activities of the 'Bridge Street Gang' were at their peak in prosecuting blasphemy in 1821. The Carliles went to gaol; so did Wooler and Edmonds and Davison. But in the early twenties prosperity and higher prices—the *Black Dwarf* sold at sixpence and the *Register* at a shilling—robbed them of their influence, and, in part, of their encouragement. The *Black Dwarf* continued until 1824, writing letters to the Yellow Bonze, bludgeoning the ministers, the Church, the bench, and the Whigs, listing the boroughmongers, praising Bentham, and crying up reform. Cobbett never stopped, but his circulation was tiny, and the *Register* was of little importance until the poor law fight in the thirties.

Opportunity was to come again, but the revived and more threatening radicalism of the thirties and forties was met by new and more confident opponents, who had learned to respect radicalism, and who could take the offensive through established organs and with a positive philosophy.

CHAPTER III

A NEW APPROACH

1820–1848

THE thirties were confronted with what Carlyle called the condition-of-England question. The terrible insecurity of a fluctuating economy, a new and often brutal discipline, a dismal life in squalid towns—these are facts which undoubted progress, even among considerable segments of the working classes, and the brilliance of the age do little to relieve. Both sides in the struggle resorted to expedients and makeshifts. The middle and upper classes, when they recognized the problem, tried various sorts of reform and investigation; but even the most radical and eventually triumphant Benthamite-Chadwickian solutions managed to infuriate some of those on—and in good part for—whom they worked.[1] The working classes too had to experiment with problems hard to express and harder to solve. They wavered between political and economic action; they struck in 1825, burned ricks and smashed machinery in 1830, united in and felt cheated by the reform struggle of 1832, turned with new enthusiasm to the continuing trade union movement, and were forced by government repression to the points of the Charter, with excursions into plug-pulling and violence. They rioted, petitioned, marched, organized, quarrelled, and usually lost. These developments have been widely explored and in main outline are part of common historical knowledge; exploration and refinement continue in a picture still far from satisfactory. There is no space here for details. It is enough to refer in passing to the matrix, and move on to one aspect of the activity of the working classes. They also read.

Benbow told a meeting of the National Union of the Working Classes in 1832 that they could no longer suffer themselves to be slaves. 'Their rulers, unfortunately for themselves, had taught them to read, and they now knew there was no actual superiority between man and man. . . .'[2] Charles Knight considered that working people having been taught to read and consequently to think had loosed a new power in society that could not be stopped, although, he added significantly, it might be given direction. Samuel Smiles pointed out that Chartism was no mere 'ebullition' of public opinion, but the result of causes operating over a half-century, helped on by Lancaster, Cobbett, and the reform struggle; above all, 'the diffusion of knowledge by means of a cheap press, has endowed it with increasing power and influence.' The *Spectator*, too, saw that the disease was 'universal and organic,' one that came of teaching people to read and neglecting their wellbeing, or, to put it another way, one that rose from the incompatibility of democratic newspapers, which government could not suppress, with near-starvation wages.[3]

The works of Paine were still important during this period; to that the advertisements in the *Poor Man's Guardian* and other working class journals testify abundantly. Cobbett's pamphlets sold well, too, and there was a great distribution of socialist and co-operative literature. But it was periodical publication that carried the day, helped on by technological advance, cheapness, and the inestimable value of present and often sensational appeal. The success of one journal would call many similar ones into a brief existence, and the *Times Handlist* is strewn with the wrecks. However much the upper classes might lament the frivolous nature of some of the periodical productions, it was the unstamped radical press that most worried them. Estimates of circulation were printed in the *Standard* in 1833. Hetherington's *Poor Man's Guardian* was given as 16,000, his *Destructive* as 8,000.[4] Figures in the thousands were certainly alarming to Tories who read them in their paper; they were alarming to Whigs and Radicals as well. The Whig attempts at repression are perhaps the strongest testimony. Prosecutions of publishers and vendors of the unstamped reached a peak in the early thirties. Knight's *Companion to the Newspaper* opposed the stamp tax, but not the prosecutions under the law, which he thought were not severe enough. The impolitic law 'lets loose upon us a great many of the evils that some persons dread from the licentiousness of the press, without any of the advantages of the cheaper, and therefore more extended, diffusion of political knowledge.'[5] James Mill wrote to Brougham, 3 September, 1832, deprecating

> the illicit cheap publications, in which the doctrines of the right of the labouring people, who say they are the only producers, to all that is produced, is very generally preached. The alarming nature of this evil you will understand when I inform you that these publications are superseding the Sunday newspapers, and every other channel through which the people might get better information. . . . I am sure it is not good policy to give the power of teaching the people exclusively to persons violating the law, and of such desperate circumstances and character that neither the legal nor the moral sanction has sufficient hold upon them. The only effectual remedy is to remove the tax which gives them this deplorable power.[6]

With the crushing of the Grand National Consolidated Trades Union and the return of good times, the circulation of the ultra-radical unstamped press declined, while the reduction of the stamp duty in 1836 made it unprofitable for them to evade the law and so denied newspapers to the very poorest classes, to whom a penny made a great deal of difference.[7] But in the forties the old alarm recurred, for there were more publications than ever. Tremenheere's reports, well into the fifties, continued to give prominence to the wide circulation in the mining districts of fiction and cheap politically upsetting papers. His remarks show the prevalent confusion in upper class opinion of socialism, atheism, and immorality, and indicate the extent of the fiction craze. The imitations of French *feuilletons* were quite as bad in his view as the imitations of French politics after 1848.

In 1850 he made a collection of periodicals circulating at a penny or three halfpence in Wednesbury and Bilston, Staffordshire; of the fifteen, seven 'were written in a good spirit, though containing portions of very inferior novels and tales . . . which would be more likely to lower the taste and injure the morals of the young than to carry any sound instruction'; while eight were hostile either to the institutions or the religion of the country. Publications in the latter class were increasing in circulation, and their advertisements showed that there were thirteen such periodicals, published chiefly in London, though not all circulated in that particular neighbourhood. The next year he bought all the periodicals sold at one shop in Newcastle and found out their weekly circulation: nine 'infidel and chartist' circulated 1,612; one 'chartist only' 600; four 'hostile to present institutions and of immoral tendency,' 1,656; and three 'religious and moral, and containing useful information,' 688. Their circulation too was increasing, ' and, indeed, the ability with which they are written, and the boldness of their attacks on revealed religion, and on our whole social system, are calculated to make them very attractive to young and inquiring minds.'[8]

The alarm over what the working classes were reading was very like the alarm in the earlier periods; but the threat was increasingly regarded as something to be met by education, or at least by what then passed for education. The education the people were to receive was clearly not to equip them for free enquiry; rather, it was the education of which James Mill wrote—the implanting in the mind, through custom or through pain and pleasure, an invariable sequence and association of ideas which would conduce in the end to the happiness of all. Mill hoped that in time the labouring class would be able to attain to a very high degree of knowledge, but only so much time could be devoted to acquiring intelligence as could be abstracted from labour. School attendance should be extended into adolescence, but meanwhile was limited and capricious. Working life began very early, and schools in any event could teach little more than the elements. The solution seemed to lie in the precious hours of leisure, and in the existence of an apparent desire for knowledge and the reading ability to acquire it.'[9]

The Mechanics' Institutions of the twenties were efforts to organize advanced education of the type that Mill intended; but, despite the enthusiasm of their founders and some notable successes, the movement was a sad failure. Some institutions were defeated by the apathy of working men who understandably did not care to spend their little leisure in study. In several cases they were torn apart by management struggles between middle class and working class groups. In others, an avoidance of entertainment or the frequent exclusion of politics alienated men who might otherwise have joined, while basic deficiencies in elementary education among those who did come meant that working men stayed away more and more. Infiltration from above turned many of them into middle class clubs—'exhibition rooms of local vanity and drowsy essay reading '—which quite belied their name.[10] Clearly the chief resources of the educators were self-instruction and the press; effective education, for the time being, had to be 'informal.'

This notion underlay most of the efforts to be examined in subsequent chapters. A writer in the *Edinburgh*, replying to an attack on Brougham's *Practical Observations*, pointed out that lectures might help to excite the few who attended, but 'the main reliance . . . of all who desire the improvement of the body of the people, must ever be on books.' Scott's friend, James Simpson, an advocate and writer active in educational movements, found in useful and entertaining knowledge as cheap as coarse paper and in lectures the means of bringing some enlightenment to those who certainly could not again be made children or be brought into advanced schools. The Leeds Popular Instruction Society stated as its aim to keep young people, after they had left school, from vicious and degrading pastimes, and to carry on the incomplete work of education by giving them the opportunity to read; reading rooms were to be scattered about the town, furnished with the universally desired newspapers, and supplied with books by a central organization. No more explicit statement of this view could be wanted than that in the prospectus of a small publication projected by Sir G. S. MacKenzie, of Coul, in Ross-shire:

> It is quite evident that several causes concur to render *schools* to a great degree inoperative. Labourers cannot attend them; nor can household servants, among which class there is more vice than may be generally suspected. There are many in these classes who can read; but there is a general feeling among them, that printed tracts thrust upon them, are so thrust from some sinister design. Gratuitous distribution will not do; it is neglected or despised; and no wonder, when the usual quality of what has been gratuitously

distributed is considered. We must begin anew; and the following method is proposed:—Let knowledge be offered at the cheapest possible rate; that is, as much of it as a very low rate can purchase. A tract without a price is not valued; but if a thing be bought, it is put to use. Do not insist on its being bought; do not thrust it on the people, but simply put it in their power, letting them know it is to be had. Now, it is observed, that the lowest class, and numbers, too, of that class immediately above, are exceedingly eager to purchase things that are hawked about the streets, such as accounts of executions and last speeches, murders, shipwrecks, and the like. The quantity of vice, trash, falsehood, and mischief that gets thus into circulation is infinitely greater than is commonly imagined. Let this method be extensively tried for disseminating physical, moral, and religious knowledge among the lowest of the people, and we hope and trust they will become more intelligent, more moral, and more religious. But the order must be as above. Let them first be tempted to purchase a regular halfpenny weekly journal, by its containing something amusing and attractive; and let it gradually come to contain a considerable proportion of sound instruction. This last will in no long time come to be relished and demanded. As soon as the circulation shall have been fairly established, by thus gradually tempting the people to read first for rational amusement and then for instruction, regular systematic instruction, including theological, may be mingled with entertainment. Those who can read may be induced to teach others who cannot; and for promoting this desire, alphabets and lessons may be distributed along with the Journal. There are thousands who may be willing to learn, who either have no opportunity, or who are too old to relish the formal discipline of a school; and it is inconceivable to what extent the influence of private example diffuses itself.[11]

Although the development of public libraries did not begin until well after the passing of the act of 1850, the previous two decades had seen a considerable development in small libraries set up in factories or collieries, in villages, and in Mechanics' Institutions. The itinerating libraries organized around Haddington in East Lothian by Samuel Brown from 1817 attracted considerable attention on the part of educational reformers. While such libraries attracted large numbers of artisans and mechanics, who did some serious reading, they cannot be said to have been unqualified successes. Even the small subscriptions usually required were some hindrance; the books, never very numerous, usually came from the Religious Tract Society, the S.P.C.K., or similar sources, or were cast-offs, which were either useless or soon exhausted. It was estimated, for example, that in Mechanics' Institutions' libraries, there might be only four or five hundred useful volumes out of a thousand. Then, too, library rules often excluded theology and politics, and it was in the latter subject that many workmen were primarily interested. Their interest might be aroused at first, but soon transferred or lost; indeed, to supply the deficiency, small libraries were sometimes formed in public houses.[12]

In turning to consider the strictly 'informal' means of education through popular literature, one immediately encounters the celebrated Society for the Diffusion of Useful Knowledge. As some of the publications of that organization will be considered in detail later, and because its reputation has been and is so great, some space must be devoted to a general examination of its activity. The material for such an estimate lies largely in the papers of the Society in University College, London. The destruction of its library during the war has made it impossible to go through all the papers of the Society, some of which will not be available for several years; this means a serious gap, particularly in the minute books. But the general correspondence directed to the Society from its members and friends, publishers and authors, is available; and, while some questions in the story might be answered through the examination of other manuscript material, the letters are in themselves quite enough to make a categorical estimate of the Society's influence possible.

When Peacock decided to satirize the S.D.U.K. in *Crotchet Castle*, he called it the Steam Intellect Society. He probably did not realize how truly perceptive that title was, for the Society was, at least in two respects, exactly like a steam engine—it was noisy, and it was inefficient. It was noisy because it had among its membership, at least in the early years, many of the most celebrated public men of the time; its chairman was Lord Brougham, who was not in any event a quiet person; and its second and principal publisher was Charles Knight. Both men were sedulous in their care for the Society's living and posthumous reputation. It was noisy, too, because it captured the imagination of that portion of the public which believed strongly in the education—and educability—of the working classes, so its reputation—aside from the working class press who could not be presumed to know—was generally favourable. Its reputation is still favourable; some modern historians have managed to commend it to their readers, not only as an admirable attempt, which it may have been, but also as an admirable accomplishment, which it certainly was not.[13]

The noise began with Brougham's celebrated pamphlet *Practical Observations upon the Education of the People*, which went through twenty editions within a year of its publication in 1825. Assuming, like Mill, the necessary 'informality' of education, he finds the chief impediments in money and time. 'To the first belongs the difficulty of obtaining those books and instructors which persons in easier circumstances can command; and to the second it is owing that the same books and instructors are not adapted to them, which suffice to teach persons who have leisure to go through the whole course of any given branch of science.' The solution lay in cheap publications. By lifting the taxes on paper, by printing closely, and by using coarse paper, work already begun could be carried further; moreover, by publishing in numbers, one might attract the working man who could easily save twopence or even sixpence a week. And, with an enthusiasm he perhaps regretted later, Brougham, not yet Lord Chancellor, went on to urge such publications on all subjects, including general and party politics and political economy.

The Society was organized in the next year. The propectus began with an explicit statement of its purpose, 'the imparting of useful information to all classes of the community, particularly to such as are unable to avail themselves of experienced teachers, or may prefer learning by themselves.' The plan was to issue each month two thirty-two page treatises, equal to one hundred ordinary pages, with wood engravings and tables, to sell for sixpence. Reductions in price were available for reading societies, Mechanics' Institutions, and education committees. A subscriber was entitled to a copy of each tract on publication and was permitted to purchase twelve or more at considerable reduction for gratuitous distribution. The list of proposed subjects came largely from natural philosophy, but also included aspects of 'intellectual philosophy,' ethics, political philosophy, history, and biography. Brougham was chairman, Lord John Russell, vice-chairman, W. E. Tooke, treasurer, and Thomas Coates, secretary. Baldwin and Cradock were chosen as the first publishers; Charles Knight joined the Society in 1828.[14] Provincial committees were set up, and the first numbers of the *Library of Useful Knowledge* were published.

That series was to be devoted almost entirely to the natural sciences and to biography. At Knight's suggestion another series, the *Library of Entertaining Knowledge*, was started for less abstruse matters, a form of competition Baldwin was not particularly happy about.[15] The other major activities, begun later, were the *Penny Magazine*, the *Penny Cyclopaedia*, booklets for farmers, a successful series of maps, and a very successful series of almanacs. The *Penny Cyclopaedia*, it seems certain, circulated largely among middle class persons; and, while the maps and almanacs undoubtedly did reach down into the working classes, they could hardly be the vehicles for much instruction. Occasional productions aside, the Society really must be judged on the basis of its two series of numbers and on the *Penny Magazine*.

In the early summer of 1828, Knight toured the manufacturing districts of the North of England to encourage the establishment of local committees; his letters to Coates give considerable information on circulation. Although sanguine about the reception of the plan and its future success, in Manchester he found 'considerable difficulties' in arousing the interest of persons deeply engrossed in their business affairs for a project which did not excite much 'local or personal feeling,' while the Society's publications were little known among the working classes. At Leeds, he thought from booksellers' answers that perhaps fifty copies of the *L.U.K.* were sold, 'some to the working classes, but principally to those of the middle and upper classes'; later he thought the figure of 125 to represent the Leeds sale. In Sheffield, he wrote on 22 June, he had enthusiastic co-operation from a Mr. Abraham who helped to introduce the treatises into neighbouring towns; four copies were taken by the Mechanics' Library at Sheffield, and about forty were sold in the town. From Nottingham he wrote on 26 June that about 250 were sold there, a greater number in proportion to population than in any other town he had visited. But, he wrote the next day, in Leicester not twenty copies were sold in a population of thirty thousand; and in Loughborough, a town of ten thousand, none of the three booksellers carried the *Library*.[16]

These not very encouraging results might be put down to the early stage of the scheme; but the correspondence with Baldwin, the publisher, shows that the circulation in 1828 was higher than it ever was thereafter. Baldwin's letters, in fact, became increasingly despondent, and his undeniable testimony pretty well contradicts the occasional good report.   As of 16 December, 1829, the preliminary treatise by Brougham had sold 33,100 copies—a remarkable figure—and the earlier scientific numbers ranged downward from 27,900 to 22,350. With the first part of 'animal mechanics' there was a rise to 25,025. Baldwin warned, though, that the abstruse treatises would fall to half their sale, were it not for the habit of taking them as they came out.[17] On 6 May, 1831, he wrote to Coates that he was hopeful that the Library would recover itself in volumes, although he was sure that the sale in numbers would decline—a certain indication of the class of purchasers. But on 1 February, 1832, he had to report that the sale was 'falling off in all directions,' and he doubted whether they could continue to print 10,000 copies, as stock was accumulating so fast. A letter of 1 May, 1832, indicated current sale as 6,000 to 6,300; No. 93, the first number of which only 10,000 were printed, had sold in all about 9,000. But the decline had to be kept secret, lest public knowledge of it accelerate the evil. The reason for Baldwin's alarm is easy to see. A pencilled note on the letter just referred to indicates that the profit to Baldwin and Cradock on a sale of five thousand was thirteen pounds, but fifty-six pounds on the second five thousand, because the

rent paid to the Society and the cost of composing and steno-
typing attached to the first five thousand. The minutes of the
Society for 15 April, 1835, indicate that the L.U.K. was still
selling four thousand, a figure which could not have encouraged Baldwin.[18]

In searching about for reasons for this startling decline,
note must be taken of several criticisms. The Society was
criticized—as one is aware from Peacock—on the grounds of
impracticality, a charge which James Mill admitted had some
validity. It was hard to get the right treatises, 'for though
subjects upon which everybody writes and talks, there are few
people who can write and talk upon them instructively.'[19]

Certainly the reluctance of the Society to take up matters of
politics and political economy affected its reputation. There
was criticism, too, of the price as too high; and some booksellers were being supplied by various persons at a reduced
price. It was also suggested that something should be done,
perhaps by amendment of the Hawkers' Licence Act or by a
more favourable discount, to permit better distribution in the
rural districts through the hawkers. But there is a report that in
1840 a hawker found no sale for the Society's pamphlets at
one-third the list price.[20]

The committee insisted on supervising every step of publication; many of the members were themselves authors; and
the MSS. and proofs were passed among the committee for
comment and correction. They were busy men, and the
Society had first claim on the attention of almost no one,
except the distracted publisher. But poor Baldwin was frequently in the dark as to what was going on; he had to deal
with charges of plagiarism, with delays in proof-reading, and
with mis-direction of copy. As a result of this cumbersome
process, no regularity of publication was attained, although
Knight had insisted on its importance during his northern
tour. Letters from booksellers, members, and friends of the
Society testify to the bad effect of irregularity. A Scottish
supporter wrote an irate letter in 1840 pointing out that the
'Outlines of History,' begun ten years previously, was not yet
completed, while the last number of the history of Rome was
dated seven years before. He thought the Society had either
to finish the treatises without delay or call in the published

numbers and refund the purchase money, as four or five shillings was of some value to a young mechanic.[21]

A charter was granted by Parliament in 1832; it was more of
the noise. The affairs of the Society were soon in a bad way.
In 1835 a thousand pounds had to be borrowed on the guarantee of some of the members; it was determined that no new
literary engagements should be entered on for two years,
except in case of 'great urgency'; and further expenses for the
L.U.K., except to complete treatises, were to be stopped by
moderate payments to engaged authors. Another loan had to
be raised in the committee when Baldwin and Cradock failed
in 1837, over two thousand pounds in debt to the Society.
By 1843 the five hundred annual subscribers to the Society had
fallen to below forty.[22] The correspondence for 1844-45 is
sad reading indeed, consisting as it does of complaints of
unfinished treatises, a few subscriptions and requests for books,
duns from suppliers, attempts at fund-raising, and a rash of
resignations from committee members. The final blow was
the utter failure of the proposed *Biographical Dictionary*, which
got through seven half-volumes of the letter A to a debt of
nearly five thousand pounds. The Society had no choice but
to wind up its affairs. The address was a brave one:

> The political circumstances of the time [1826] had much
> influence in producing its formation. It could not be other-
> wise at a time when the opinion that there was danger to
> religion and to government in the spread of knowledge was
> avowed by many, acted on by more, and generally supposed,
> whether justly or not, to be at least not discouraged by those
> at the head of the State.
>
> It needed an energetic combination, both of well known
> names and of working power, to create an effective opposi-
> tion to a principle now exploded, and which never could
> have been true except upon suppositions anything but
> advantageous to the religion and the government in support
> of which it was brought forward. If this fear of knowledge
> still existed, the Committee would hold it necessary to con-
> tinue their active operations. But it does not now exist: all
> parties at this day appeal to the reason of the people at large,
> desire them to instruct themselves, and offer them the

means. The advocates of knowledge are more powerful than their opponents ever were, and those opponents have disappeared.[23]

Given the material presently available—and minutes, account books, and the destroyed Knight papers would probably only make the impression of disaster more nearly complete —there is no doubt about the serious failure of the organization to accomplish what it set out to do. It aimed, said Knight, at instructing all classes,[24] but it is certain that, from its inception, the primary target was the working class reading public. And it seems equally certain, from the testimony adduced here, and from the publications still to be considered, that its sales among the working classes were very small and proportionally of no importance at all. Brave talk about the fulfilment of its mission does not mask its defeat. Cassell, in the fifties, was to succeed amazingly against greater competition than the Society raised in the forties; and the Chambers brothers, who set out to do the same things and did them much better, prospered. Had the Society paid less attention to the big names it considered so important, had it contented itself with less ambitious aims and less strident publicity, had it supplied working class demands for politics (impossible, of course, for middle class whigs and most radicals), and had it been properly and efficiently managed, it might have had some modest sort of success, too, and not have had to rely for its justification on the posthumous puffing of its founders and on the credulity of historians.

Still, the Society must be spared a few of its laurels. Some of the little treatises on science were adequate and probably instructed a fair number of people especially interested; the almanacs and maps were undoubtedly useful in homes and schools; and the *Penny Cyclopaedia* was of considerable importance to those who could not afford the *Britannica*. Furthermore, it was early in a new field. Its experiments in quantity publishing were striking and encouraging, and successors and competitors could learn by its mistakes.[25] But the great significance of the Society for this study—and the justification for extended treatment—is its position as the largest and most famous of the efforts to provide machinery which not only could attempt a positive indoctrination of the working classes, if used intelligently, but which also could act rapidly and with the assurance of an established reputation, when a particular crisis or social problem called for immediate ministrations from the press. Its failures in both tasks must not be overlooked; they are revealing, but subordinate. The fact of its existence, as an instrument of a confident class in a fight for opinions, has an importance it would be hard to overrate.

Abortive competitors which appeared during the early years of the S.D.U.K., such as the *National Library* or the *Library for the People* need no attention, but a little space must be devoted to the awakening of the Society for Promoting Christian Knowledge. A supplemental catalogue to their regular lists of Bibles and tracts issued after 1817, was a kind of *imprimatur* placed on works of other publishers; and the ferment of 1819 led to the setting up of an anti-infidel committee, which was revived in 1830-31 and 1838-39. But direct activity outside the religious field had to wait until 1832.

On 21st May of that year, at a special general meeting of the Society a report was read on the growing influence of the press on the minds and conduct of much of the population. The extensive sale of penny magazines was cited in proof, and the unpleasant fact noted that none of them was conducted on principles in support of established religion, while many if not most were aimed at the 'passions and prejudices of the multitude. . . .' Consequently, a Committee of General Literature was set up under the Dean of Chichester, J. W. Parker was appointed as agent, and a grant in aid was voted. The publications, always to have a Christian tendency and character, though not confined to the strict limits of Christian knowledge, were to include a series of religious tracts—a 'Library of Christian Knowledge'—school books, historical and biographical series, a scientific series with a 'decided bias' towards revelation, and a penny magazine. The latter was immediately set on foot and appeared as the *Saturday Magazine*, and the rest of the scheme was soon implemented. The minutes of the Committee indicate the usual run of acceptances and rejections: a manuscript on the effects of incendiarism was declined in 1834 as the crime was by that time infrequent; a paper on geology was rejected because it contained—hardly surprising—objectionable parts ; a history of England was amended to convey a more Christian tone. In 1835 the Committee was assimilated more closely to the parent society and its efforts were directed more to educational subjects; in 1837 the *Saturday Magazine* was completely transferred to Parker, and the Society's responsibility ceased; and after that time, being primarily a publisher of texts for National schools, the Committee ceases to be of much interest, although it is worth noting that they published a work on political economy by Whately, and that 1848 brought *A Few Words on Strikes and Combinations*, although some other works relating to the crisis of that year apparently did not get beyond consideration by the Committee.[26]

Individual publishers too set out to cater to the demand for popular educational literature, in most cases, of course, only as a subordinate part of general publishing. Along with Charles Knight in London, the best example of private enterprise in this field is that of William and Robert Chambers, who, starting in Edinburgh in the late twenties, built up a remarkably successful business. William was the effective head of the publishing firm; Robert, later famous as the author of *Vestiges of the Natural History of Creation*, was associated with him, but primarily as a writer. Their two series of *Information for the People*, the *Miscellany of Useful and Entertaining Tracts*, the *Educational Course*, and similar publications reached a circulation certainly equal to that of the treatises of the S.D.U.K. and a stability which the more publicized organization never attained. From 1832 to 1836 *Chambers's Historical Newspaper* appeared monthly in eight folio pages, sold at three halfpence, to comment on the news from a radical Whig and often unorthodox point of view. By early 1833 the paper had reached a combined London and Edinburgh printing of 28,000, but the average circulation of 10,000 hardly met expenses, so the brothers transferred their energies to other works. Abel Heywood, the Manchester bookseller, testified some years later, however, that the paper had been abandoned because of a notice served on the Chamberses for violation of the stamp laws.[27] But their most remarkable and important publication was *Chambers's Edinburgh Journal*, whose lineal descendant is still in existence.

The idea of an established, regular magazine for the growing reading public among the working classes and lower middle classes was not a new one. Patrick Colquhoun, for example, in his *Treatise on Indigence* of 1806, urged the publication of a weekly police gazette, 'to excite in the minds of the labouring people a strong sense of moral virtue, loyalty, and love of their country; to forewarn the unwary, and to arrest the hands of evil-doers by appropriate admonitions, introduced in plain and familiar language.' It would contain abstracts of acts of Parliament touching the ordinary man, 'occasional short essays, conveyed in familiar language, enlivened and rendered interesting by the introduction of narrative as often as circumstances will permit,' on sedition, treason, combinations of workmen, mobs and unlawful assemblies, on the whole catalogue of felonies, on the horrors of gaol, and on religious and moral duties like frugality and patience under adversity. The idea was put into effect in part in a publication called *Hue and Cry*, but indications are that it excited little support, apparently because it contained no news but police, and because 'dry moral essays will never interest the public mind.'[28]

To associate moral and intellectual improvement with entertainment was clearly the idea behind the *Cheap Magazine*, founded and operated with a considerable sense of mission by a strange Haddington bookseller, George Miller, in 1813-14;[29] and I am certain that Miller's little journal helped to inspire Charles Knight. The son of a bookseller, Knight became editor of the *Windsor and Eton Express* in 1812 and rose in time to a commanding position in the field of popular literature. In January, 1814, he wrote to a friend outlining a project for a cheap weekly work—heavily moral and religious—'for the use of the industrious part of the community, who have neither money to buy, nor leisure to read, bulky and expensive books.' But his effective start was brought about by an article in his paper in 1819 in which he called attention to the new and growing power of literacy 'entrusted to the great mass of the working people,' which was so mercilessly exploited by seditious and infidel writers under a brilliant leader, Cobbett. He urged that a man of genius learn the lessons that the radical writers had to teach and add what they had thrown away, 'the power of directing the affections to what is reverend and beautiful in national manners and institutions.' The article caught the attention of Edward Hawke Locker, an admiralty civil servant who lived in Windsor, and the two men founded *The Plain Englishman*, which ran for three years, from 1820 to 1822.

Each issue contained sermons, moral tales, poems, some entertaining articles, and a few scientific items. The second of its three sections, however, reflected the troubled background. This section, ' The British Patriot,' made a strong appeal to love of country and to the danger of change. There was a series on great naval battles, another on important historical events, still another on 'popular law,' in which the flavour of Colquhoun's recommendations still persists. Knight saw later that, in the panic of the times, he, like his contemporaries, had overlooked the injustice which led to agitation, and that his first periodical effort was 'dragging a chain of doubtful timidity.' Further, at fifty pages it was too large, and its price of a shilling was too high. It could have reached down surely no farther than the highest ranks of the artisans, if that far; and it stood little chance of ' an extensive natural sale amongst the young and newly half-educated. A Weekly Penny or Twopenny Sheet, such as I had proposed in 1812, might have had a better chance of success, but still a very small chance.' The newspapers offered headier brew. Lack of encouragement on both sides brought the venture to a close; there was insufficient reading, insufficient patronage, and apparently some downright opposition from 'one great society,' perhaps the S.P.C.K., which comes in for hard words from Knight elsewhere. By 1828 Knight had realized, though he was never able entirely to act on it, that no scheme of this type could be successful unless addressed directly to the intended audience, without dependence on patronage or on free, and so suspect, distribution by the upper classes.[30]

The late twenties saw the ground better prepared. For one thing, technological advance had made cheap quantity printing possible. The Fourdrinier paper machine and the Cowper and Applegarth cylinder press created something of a revolution in printing, for, with manual labour, no matter how good, working round the clock, impressions of fifty to eighty thousand could not be put out. But in 1835 a foreign visitor watched with amazement twenty steam presses turning out the *Penny Magazine* each at a thousand sheets per hour. By the forties the *Family Herald*, which attained an enormous circulation, boasted of a new type-setting machine which allowed the composition and printing of ten thousand copies so that the last sheet could be read 170 miles south and 300 miles north of London within twenty-four hours—a development which the spread of the railway and the reform of the Post Office helped on.[31] Again, the twenties had seen the considerable success of the scientific *Mechanics' Magazine*, started in 1824; while a whole host of competitors revealed a popularity and occasional misguidedness which led directly in 1832 to the founding of three great weekly magazines.

Chambers's Journal began publication in February. 'It may be presumed,' said William Chambers years later, 'to have been under an ardent conviction of [the] real and fancied imperfections, in the miscellaneous crowd of cheap sheets, that were appearing during the troublous period of 1831, that the writer of this paper formed the resolution to adventure as a caterer of popular literature, at a price to render it generally accessible.' The first twelve numbers were confined pretty much to Scotland, with 31,000 copies printed; a separate London impression was then started from plates stereotyped in Edinburgh, and the circulation soon doubled. At the beginning of the second year the sale was 50,000 and increasing; at the beginning of 1845, the sale approached 90,000.[32]

The first issue of the S.D.U.K.'s *Penny Magazine* appeared at the end of March. It was started at the suggestion of Matthew Davenport Hill, one of the most active of the Society's supporters, and edited by Charles Knight. Sold at a penny, a halfpenny cheaper than *Chambers's*, and provided with woodcuts, it soon reached the quite phenomenal sale of 200,000 in weekly numbers and monthly parts, a figure Knight calculated to mean a million readers. By the mid-forties, however, its sale had dropped to 40,000 and barely covered the costs of production.[33] The *Saturday Magazine* of the S.P.C.K. followed three months later and was very much like the *Penny Magazine* in form and content, except that the former, of course, paid greater attention to religion. Its regular sale was reported as about 80,000 in 1833; but, in 1836, Parker, the publisher, in prosecuting an employee for stealing several hundred numbers to sell as waste paper, stated that the weekly publication figure was 20,000, many of which were sent abroad. In 1837 the whole responsibility for the magazine was transferred, not without unpleasantness, to Parker; and in 1844 he closed the venture down.[34] In the next year Knight took over the *Penny Magazine* from the moribund S.D.U.K., and it continued an attenuated existence until June, 1846.

Both journals were motivated by a sense of crisis. The *Saturday Magazine*, relatively uninfected by new ideas, continued to harp on old themes amid the platitudinous improving knowledge. Knight's opening address, on the other hand, is a perfect reflection of the approach outlined in Mill. He hoped, by enlarging 'the range of observation, to add to the store of facts, to awaken the reason, and to lead the imagination into agreeable and innocent trains of thought, [which] may assist in the establishment of a sincere and ardent desire for information: and [to] prepare the way for the reception of more elaborate and precise knowledge. . . .'[35]

On the cessation of the *Penny Magazine* Knight's address was unsparing in its denunciation of the cheap sensational sheets, employing sweated labour, and diffusing 'a moral miasma through the land, in the shape of the most vulgar and brutal fiction'; against such competition amongst the least informed who most required sound knowledge, efforts such as his and Chambers's had little chance.[36] That development alone is perhaps enough to explain the failure of the magazines to penetrate the groups for which they were primarily intended. The initial success of the *Penny Magazine* was certainly not maintained; the *Saturday Magazine* probably circulated only among religious families; and *Chambers's Journal* for 6 February, 1847, pointed out that, of its circulation of about 80,000, 50,000 were issued in monthly parts and so presumably for the upper classes. This meant, they went on to say, a failure in their object; papers intended for the cottage went to the drawing room. B. F. Duppa, an active member of the S.D.U.K. admitted in 1839 that the *Penny Magazine*, like others of the Society's publications, 'have only, to a limited extent, reached the humblest classes of this country; but other classes have been found who were in want of the information contained in these works, and have benefited by them.' W. E. Hickson told the Select Committee on Newspaper Stamps that he had never known a working man, dependent on weekly wages, to take in the *Penny Magazine* for any length of time; *Chambers's* he took himself. He did recall having seen a copy of the latter in a cottage near Newcastle, but he thought its circulation lay chiefly among small shopkeepers, and certainly not among the portion of the working class earning under sixteen shillings per week.[37]

Chambers's Journal suggested faulty distribution as a factor in the failure—that booksellers found the parts less troublesome than the numbers, or that they were simply supine. There were certainly other causes, chief among which was the material. The initial impact of the *Penny Magazine* was certainly due to its illustrations; G. J. Holyoake recalled having given some copies of it to a fiddler in Derbyshire who had never before seen an illustrated paper, and 'they proved as valuable as glass beads in dealing with Indians.'[38] But James Simpson thought that both the *Penny Magazine* and *Chambers's* required for any real benefit more early elementary instruction, both intellectual and moral, than was usually available among the groups to whom the papers were originally intended to appeal. C. D. Collett said in 1851 that he thought the Chamberses would admit that they were handicapped by not being able to include news, while he considered that the *Penny Magazine* failed to circulate among many operatives because they demanded politics and resented the fact that it was allowed to circulate, while the unstamped press, which gave them what they wanted, was persecuted. Bulwer Lytton had made this point earlier, insisting that the *Penny Magazine* did not go so far as supposed to counteract the violent press, as men anxious to better their condition were always interested in politics. The corrective for bad politics was not only good literature, but good politics.[39]

A distinction in favour of *Chambers's Journal* must be made. Though slightly more expensive than the others and never provided with illustrations, its circulation increased and then remained, if modest, fairly steady; and some of that circulation certainly did reach the upper levels of the working classes. Further, the paper was treated with much more respect by the working class press and their sympathizers.[40] The *Journal* always included a tale; it admitted poetry; and it did not shrink from taking up, not news, but political and economic matters of current interest. If the conclusions which it put forward were not those acceptable for the most part to the working classes, at least the fact that it discussed the matters at all gave the impression that no attempt was being made to keep things from the readers.[41] *Chambers's Journal* is still readable today. It is not exciting reading, but neither is it vapid or silly.

The other two journals can excite in the modern reader little but disgust. They are largely compilations of quaint facts and descriptions of various animals, buildings, and natural phenomena. Knight was probably quite right in contending that most of his audience were looking only for relaxation and did not want to have to labour to acquire facts that they might be interested in.[42] Nevertheless, it is incontestable that the contents of his journal, and of his religious competitor's, must soon have palled on any except children, when there was more exciting reading, particularly fiction, available. The advertisement at the end of the last volume of the *Penny Magazine* points out that it had been 'a safe Miscellany, in which all classes might find *much* information and *some* amusement.' Those proportions were clearly wrong. Sometimes, too, the contents leave an inescapable impression of haste, thoughtlessness, and no small amount of desperation. After all, it is no easy task to go through fourteen years of weekly publication continually hunting for some animal or place or person that has not been discussed before. The *Poor Man's Guardian* sneered at its 'useful' knowledge—accounts of Charing Cross (ironically, written by William Hone), the antiquity of beer, the lost comet, and woodcuts of 'the bear, the dormouse, the swallow, etc. . . .,' and posed a choice between knowledge 'calculated to make you free . . . or namby-pamby stuff published expressly to stultify the minds of the working people and make them the spiritles- and unresisting victims of a system of plunder and oppression.'[43] Beneath the exasperation there is much truth. The *Penny Magazine* neither drove out bad publications nor cultivated a better taste in reading among the working classes. A middle class whig view of what the working classes *should* read, its sole distinction, woodcuts aside, is to have attained a remarkably large circulation—for a very short time.

In the recurring social and political crises of the thirties and forties, as will appear in later chapters, the old-fashioned approach dominant in attempts to reach the working class reader before 1820 was still in evidence. Essentially negative or admonitory, it continued to reveal a lack of understanding on the part of its practitioners of what was happening in British society. These publications, however, are no longer a primary concern to this study. The real problem lies with the elements of middle class Britain who realized to some extent the magnitude and meaning of the working class movements, and who had the confidence and the imagination to attempt positive solutions, in the press as well as in legislation. The history of these attempts is another series of experiments and failures, both more significant than those of earlier writers. The failures will be the measure of an unexpected difference between classes, even between middle class and working class wings of the radical movement. The experiments will be the measure of the concern and faith of their projectors.

This chapter has dealt with the establishment of new machinery for the 'informal' education of the working classes. The existence of other smaller schemes than those discussed here, the projection or organization of lesser or local tract societies or popular magaines emphasize the extent to which the need was felt in a class motivated by complementary feelings of victory and insecurity. Some of the projects were results of a strong missionary instinct, some were efforts of relatively astute businessmen, but that makes no difference to the issue. The need was there; the only trouble was with the audience.

It is not, however, enough to discuss the machinery, to point out how far it failed to accomplish its goals, or even to suggest, as I have tried to do, some of the reasons for the failures. The more important question is one of the ideas which it was hoped to put across by means of this machinery. 'Informal' education was applied in many fields. One of them was simply that of wholesome, interesting information, either for its own sake, or to keep enquiring minds from more embarrassing questions; and some indication of the results has been suggested in connexion with the *Penny Magazine*. Another was the cheap publication of great works of literature, which involved an entirely different set of machinery and different problems, which can hardly be discussed here. Still another field, and in many ways the most successful, was in science, both theoretical and applied. The great majority of the S.D.U.K tracts, the *Mechanics' Magazine*, and the Mechanics' Institutions for the most part, belong in this category. But again the subject is one which demands separate treatment.

Socially the most significant field of 'informal' education was that relating to the political and economic conflicts between the classes and to the recurring crises which gave to the thirties and forties so disturbing an aspect. It is necessary, then, to examine the problem of political indoctrination in general—a delicate issue whose outcome will throw further light on the nature and weaknesses of the machinery of indoctrination and point up vital conflicts in ideas between middle class and working class. Then it will be possible to turn to an examination of some specific attempts to remove 'social ignorance' in the hope that 'popular tumults' might be avoided.

CHAPTER IV

THE DANGERS OF POLITICS

I T was not easy to escape from politics in nineteenth-century Britain. It filled the newspapers; it was a principal means of mass entertainment. Economic and social protests almost invariably turned to political expression: it was the programme preached by reformers to an unenfranchised populace; it was the bias from which none of the industrial movements has been able to remain immune. Given this remarkable concern, it would seem that no field called more for the intervention of popular educators; yet in no field, with the possible exception of religion, were the popular educators more timid. The exception cannot be made unqualified, as many of the politically timid had no scruples about the teaching of popularized science, the questions of which were beginning to challenge revelation. Perhaps in politics the thin edge of the wedge was most threatening.

Working class advancement of their own political education went far beyond mere reading of newspapers. Political tract societies were set up for propaganda and education; the circulation of literature by co-operative missions and societies was immense. Chartists formed classes and tract societies. The Durham Political Union in 1840 urged that classes be made real instruments of instruction, and that members study the 'works of history, and especially the history of our own country, discussing its great events philosophically, not as mere matters of fact, but noting their bearing on our present state, and tracing the entire chain of development by which the constitution of society has been unfolded. . . .'[1] And advertisements in working class papers are filled with titles of reprinted standard radical works.

That religious reactionaries should have opposed the teaching of politics in any way is to be expected. Thus a Yorkshire clergyman, denouncing Brougham's scheme for popular education by informal means, maintained that, for every one genius whose advance would be facilitated in that way, ninety-nine lesser men would develop 'discontent, insubordination, pride, and, probably, a disbelief in revelation,' in exchange 'for the tranquillity which a happy ignorance of Political Economy and party politics was accustomed to procure them.'[2]

More progressive members of the middle class realized that there was no stopping the flood; they looked to harnessing it, to diverting it into their own channels. Brougham, in his *Practical Observations* of 1825, was unequivocal; in being so, he brought down the wrath of conservatives and stored up embarrassment for himself in future, when his own Society did not take up the challenge. Let cheap works on politics be provided, and let men exercise their choice:

> Assuredly, a country which tolerates every kind, even the most unmeasured, of daily and weekly discussion in the newspapers, can have nothing to dread from the diffusion of political doctrines in a form less desultory, and more likely to make them be both well weighed at the time, and preserved for repeated perusal.

The writer of an 1831 pamphlet demanded a counter-attack on Cobbett and Carlile. By simple and well-written pamphlets on plain political questions and free lectures on politics to the lower orders they 'would be led first to doubt, and then to desert, the principles of their self-elected leaders;—and by an honest and judicious management of the influence which they would thus acquire, the writers and lecturers of whom I speak would at length be enabled to instil into the minds of their pupils, in a gradual and almost imperceptible manner, any principles and doctrines they desired.'[3] James Phillips Kay, later Sir James Kay-Shuttleworth, wrote in 1832 that the 'ascertained truths of political science' should be taught to working men early, and 'correct political information' constantly disseminated among them; to accomplish this end, the taxes on periodical publication should be removed. When Chief Justice Tindal, in his charge to the grand jury after Frost's Rebellion in 1839, urged the diffusion of the benefits of religious instruction, the *Spectator* indicated how much more to the point it would have been, had the Chief Justice recommended the diffusion of political and social knowledge.[4]

Such are typical examples of the extremes of opinion on the subject of political education, but the significant clash did not lie between these two views. The principled and dying tory opposition to education would never have stopped the radicals, had they been able to work alone. But they needed allies, and the allies were timid.

In the concern over the relative failure of the Mechanics' Institution movement in the late thirties and early forties, there was general recognition of the disservice done to the movement by the exclusion of politics. Samuel Smiles criticized the uninteresting nature of the subjects taught, and pointed out that, after a hard day's labour, the exhausted worker sought relaxation and amusement; if he should want instruction, it would be on subjects of real interest to him, and of these politics was the chief. But politics, newspapers, and even music and similar forms of amusement were excluded from the programmes of the Mechanics' Institutions. The report on Mechanics' Institutions issued by the S.D.U.K. in 1841 contained a tardy insistence that political matters could no longer be kept from the working classes. Chartists and Socialists were active in diffusing their peculiar views in free discussions, including as well features, such as lectures on science, formerly the province of the Mechanics' Institutions alone. The number of members of Socialist institutions in London, it was pointed out, was smaller than the numbers enrolled in Mechanics' Institutions, but attendance at Socialist institutions was much greater; 'and this is believed to arise principally from the fact that the rival institution offers to the workman those things the exclusion of which from the Mechanics' Institutions (especially the right of free inquiry) renders them, if not distasteful, at least uninteresting to him.'[5]

In the previous chapter it was shown that the prospectus of the S.D.U.K. listed several subjects in the political field to which treatises were to be devoted. Place was certain that political treatises were intended as part of the Society's activity; in his first enthusiasm over the scheme, he placed political treatises first, reflecting his own estimate of their importance.[6] In 1827 the *Edinburgh Review*, whose references to the S.D.U.K. were inspired, if not always written, by Brougham, commented that no opposition to the Society could be expected while it confined itself to natural science and ancient history; but, once modern history and particularly the history of England were approached, objections would surely appear. Yet the writer looked forward not only to history, but to separate treatises, 'avowedly intended to unfold the doctrine of civil policy in all its branches,' and he anticipated the greatest benefits to the country from such publications, if proper candour and justice were displayed.[7]

The Society made some partial attempts to teach political economy, and its *ad hoc* publications on machinery, combinations, and poor laws, turned out to meet specific crises, will be examined later. But the series of treatises on morals, politics, and political economy promised in the prospectus and expected with hopes or fears by everyone never appeared. Hardly a political word is to be found in the *Penny Magazine*, which sought rather to substitute for politics than to teach it. And an incident of 1833 is most instructive. Place had given his support to a Mr. Vialls who wanted to open a reading room for mechanics, and who applied to the secretary of the S.D.U.K. for a grant of books. The secretary replied with a negative on the grounds that the rooms were too small and that food was to be served; but a paragraph in the report of the Mechanics' Library Committee made it apparent that the Committee also disapproved of the presence of novels and newspapers.[8] And when one of the Society's authors, a Mrs. Busk, who had compiled the history of Spain and Portugal in the *L.U.K.*, found her 'Letter to the People of England' rejected, she wrote indignantly to Coates:

> I had no suspicion of the Society's objection to politics. I wrote the Letter with the especial wish that they should adopt it conceiving no species of knowledge to be more useful to the great body of the working classes, than an explanation of the importance to themselves of maintaining some of those institutions against which demagogues most excite them. I am almost tempted to ask, can an argument against extravagant hopes and delusions be called politics?[9]

The Society's failure in the political field was roundly criticized. Correspondents took them to task; the *Poor Man's Guardian* blasted Brougham for hypocrisy; the *Monthly Repository* damned them; and John Wade, the author of the *Black Book*, suggested delicately that the treatises had been principally on physical science, 'probably from the difficulty of fixing the precise standard of utility in the dissemination of the truths of moral and political philosophy.'[10]

The Society's address on its disbanding in 1846 stated that, at the outset, they had determined to avoid religion and government as topics, 'with obvious prudence.' Given the political excitement of the time, and the division even among friends of education on the best means of adjusting the disharmony in the country, 'any interference with theology or politics would have endangered the existence of a union which demanded the most cordial co-operation from all who wished well to the cause.'

A similar suggestion was contained in the defence of the conduct of the Society offered by a member, Alfred Fry, to objections made during a discussion at two meetings of the Birmingham Mechanics' Institution in 1832. William Pare, an active Owenite, led the attack on the Society. He admitted that the *L.U.K.* contained admirable treatises; but, he insisted, the Society had shirked the most important matter for instruction, politics; and that aspect of politics which they had essayed, political economy, had been treated in a manner that was partial, ill-informed, and even mocking. By political knowledge he explained, he did not mean partisan discussions of current issues, but the 'great principles of the social connection, which intimately concerned the working classes.'

In his replies, Fry insisted that politics had always been excluded from the Society's plan, that its introduction had never been contemplated, a statement quite untrue. To complain of the absence of politics, he said, was much like criticizing an exhibition of water-colours for containing no paintings in oils. The Society had done well; it had accustomed people to use their understandings; it had set the example of cheap publication; and it deserved credit.

Still, the Society's works, it was said, do not circulate among the working classes. He was sorry for that; but if those classes chose to neglect the publications in question, it was not the fault of the Society. Suppose he were to say to a working man, 'You spend two shillings in gin, why not spend one of them on a Working Man's Companion?' 'Oh! it contains errors.' 'It may be so (he would reply), but nothing is free from error and it is your duty to lay hold on truth as far as you can, when it is offered to you.' As to the fact that the works in question were supported by the middle classes,—it was doubtless true. He who read these books became one of the middle class. It was the middle class who supported everything, because they had all the industry and all the intelligence. There was, it was true, a difference in the *luck* of different persons. By *luck* he understood the occurrence of events beyond our calculation.

After this rather unhappy argument, he suggested that the inclusion of politics as a subject would have been disruptive.

If it had been found that five thousand persons might be benefitted by an association which excluded politics, and only two hundred if politics made a part of its plan, it was clearly advisable that politics should be excluded. Nevertheless, if the two hundred thought politics necessary, they were free to form a separate association. Political economy, however, occupied a considerable part of the Society's attention; but Mr. Pare differed from the Society on certain points. Perhaps Mr. P. differed from the majority of mankind. In the present instance, however, he had only asserted that there were errors published; he did not specify what the errors were. In fine, it was his firm opinion that the Society had chosen the most beneficial course. No one could read the *Entertaining Series* without becoming a better man than he was before he commenced the perusal.—The volumes on the Insect Creation alone were full of the deepest interest, and gave a high, refined, and softened tone to the mind; while the study of politics had the effect of hardening the heart. The political student seemed to be always in armour.[11]

The division within the counsels of the Society, implied in this passage, becomes quite clear in the seemingly reliable information contained in a powerful attack on the Society in the *Westminster Review*. The members of the Society, the writer charged, were completely ignorant of their audience. As all the people whom the Society really intended to reach lived by wages, the doctrine of wages should have been the foundation of all other instruction. Beyond that they should have been taught the importance of property and government, the rules of morality, obedience to the law, frugality, kindness, and beneficence. But what did the Society do, when faced with an ignorant and prejudiced, combining and rick-burning public in 1827? It produced a confused and erroneous preliminary treatise, tracts on hydrostatics and pneumatics, and promised 'to a people ignorant of every thing most intimately connected with their welfare . . . two treatises . . . on the Polarisation of Light, and another on the Rigidity of Cordage!'

Brougham, the writer maintained, misled by a desire for power, nullified his educational efforts by an alliance with the aristocracy and clergy. How could any society function which included such diverse persons as Sir James Scarlett, James Mill, Captain Basil Hall, Warburton, and Brougham? The best men were the busiest, and the schemes fell into the hands of the meddling, truckling, and prudent. It was not, then, that the Society, after all its bold statements, *could* not disseminate knowledge among the people; it was that they *would* not.[12]

At the end of 1837, Brougham called the attention of the Committee to the absence of 'all intellectual, ethical, or political subjects from the publications of the Society.' There were some negotiations about a constitutional history, but the only result was the *Political Philosophy*, written by Brougham himself. It was not a success, and the final address of the Society explained the failure in this way:

Six years ago, when the circumstances of the time seemed favourable, the Committee so far departed from the usual practice as to publish a series of political treatises drawn up by their Chairman, forming the only accessible work in which the existing constitutions of the principal countries of the world are described both in principle and detail. But the event showed strong reason to conclude that the part of the public which called out for politics wanted, not knowledge of the facts nor lessons of experience, but only stimulus for party feeling, and materials for party discussions. The Society accordingly gave up the intention of completing the above-named series, and abandoned a work on Political Economy which had been prepared.[13]

Another instructive example of the influence of whiggism in repressing of political comment is provided by the experience of Alexander and John Bethune, the poor Scottish labourers turned authors and poets. They had the notion in 1837 of publishing a series of lectures on political, or as they called it 'popular' or 'practical,' economy; they needed money to settle their parents on a small farm, and the distress of the times seemed to them to provide a stimulus to read such a work as they proposed. The lectures were sent to a friend who approved the project and predicted success,

> provided you do not get too red-hot in your political speculations. . . . In these fiery times, we have too many wise-acres who 'sit by the fire, and presume to know what is done in the capitol.' Nor do I think that, moving in a sphere so circumscribed, you can be thoroughly qualified for such a task. But, with the talents for observation, and the power of industrious application, you possess, you are well calculated to succeed in the stern, practical topic you have chosen.

To this letter Alexander Bethune replied that their politics were not red-hot, but white-hot, for only through white-hot politics could the working classes be reached.

> Talk to them of religion, and they will put on a long face—confess that it is a thing of the greatest importance to all—and go away and forget the whole. Talk to them of education: they will readily acknowledge that 'it's a braw thing to be weel learned,' and perhaps, begin a lamentation . . . on the ignorance of the age in which they live; but they neither stir hand nor foot farther. When you are gone, they are silent on the subject, and the acknowledgment and the lamentation are with them the alpha and omega of the matter. But only speak to them of politics, and their excited countenances and kindling eyes testify in a moment

how deeply they are interested. If, moreover, you have anything new to tell them, or even a new face to put on an old story, the thing will serve them as a subject of conversation among their companions for weeks to come; and they will hardly fail to narrate the whole as faithfully as they can to their wives and families, should they have such, with the return of every evening. Politics are therefore an important feature, and an almost indispensable element in such a work. Had it consisted solely of exhortations to industry, and rules of economy, it would have been dismissed with an 'Ou-ay, it's braw for him to crack that way; but if he were whaur we are, deed he wad just hae to do as we do.' Then, with most readers, the principles which the work was intended to teach, would be at once put aside, without so much as a trial—executed according to Cupar justice, before they could even be condemned. But by mixing up the science with politics, and giving it occasionally a political impetus, a different result may more reasonably be expected. In these days, no man can be considered a patriot or a friend of the poor, who is not also a politician.

The politics they included in their draft apparently was an attack on the corn laws and on the 'servile homage which the poor are accustomed to bestow on the rich,' and an advocacy of the spread of property-holding.

The friend sent the lectures on to Thomas Murray, an active figure in early Scottish adult education, and a lecturer on political economy. Murray reacted favourably, submitted criticisms, and sent along an abstract of his own lectures as a guide. He was anxious, however, to see the work cleared of certain 'defects and excrescences' unworthy of such capable men, and he particularly wanted to cut out any 'tendency to place one great class of society in hateful opposition to another.' The Bethunes disclaimed any such intention, but eventually Murray won, and Alexander wrote him in February, 1838, that he would find the lectures entirely free from politics. Murray was now highly pleased, recommended the book to McCulloch, and thought every cotton spinner in Glasgow should have a copy of it. In the event the work was an almost total failure, and Alexander wrote to an Edinburgh friend:

We took the wrong road, however. In these days, if a man would make his way to fame, he should, in the first place, persuade people that they are not all to blame for their own poverty and misfortunes—these having been wholly brought on them by others; and, in the second place, he should arraign the government as the prime mover and the great first cause of all the misery in the country. Or he should bespatter either the Tories or the Radicals with all his might; it matters little which, provided he do it consistently, because in any way he identifies himself with a party, and is thus almost certain of success.[14]

There were institutional attempts to break through the crust of timidity. Brougham and Knight, to their credit, turned from the temporizing of the S.D.U.K. in this field to found the Society for the Diffusion of Political Knowledge in 1834. The prospectus stated that they proposed to carry into this relatively untouched field the same good work which the S.D.U.K. had done in the matter of general learning, in the hope of replacing a 'groundwork of prejudice' with a 'foundation of knowledge.' Unfortunately, with materials at present available, the brief and quiet course of this organization cannot be traced, but the form it was given is an indirect comment on its parent society. Members were to be elected by ballot, the number of acting members being limited to sixty. No individual was considered as pledged to any doctrine in a publication, or beyond a 'general concurrence in principles of peace, rational liberty, and the cause of human improvement.' Donors of ten guineas or over and authors of gratuitous treatises were to be honorary life members. And the list of members was proof that the sheep had been separated from the goats.[15] The aim was clearly at the working classes; the prospectus left no doubt of that. The Society took over the 'superintendence' of the publication of the *Companion to the Newspaper*, a venture Knight had begun in 1833 to bring together facts, to follow the course of legislation, to publicize little known measures of national improvement, and to diffuse a knowledge of the accepted principles of political economy. Originally of sixteen pages and sold at twopence, the *Companion* was raised twice in both size and price and expired at the beginning of 1837. The Society which sponsored it had quietly slipped off the scene some time before, without ever having brought a promised second periodical, *The Citizen*—to explain rights and duties under the laws—into being.

Place, Roebuck, and Hume were the moving figures of an earlier scheme for a similar society. The idea was broached in the latter part of 1831 as an organization for tract publication. Place, with characteristic thoroughness, set to figuring costs and came to the rather unhappy conclusion that the price could not be less than fourpence per tract, and 1*s*. 2*d*. for a volume of three. By the end of 1832 the plan involved a journal, of which Place and Roebuck were to be joint editors. A circular calling a meeting early in 1833 stated clearly the radicals' determination to educate their masters, thirty years before a famous whig pronouncement to that effect was made:

[The benevolent and prudent] should unhesitatingly, boldly, come forward, and to their utmost impart POLITI-CAL and MORAL knowledge to the people. Putting aside for the moment all consideration of that pure and high-minded benevolence which leads a man to do good to his fellows without any benefit accruing to himself—waiving the notice of this class of motives,—let us reflect upon the immediate influence upon our own happiness which our present conduct will exercise. If we be inert—if we let the people go on, condemned to ignorance by flagitious and imbecile rulers, what will be the result to that portion of society who now stand between the present governors of the nation and those usually called the people? Should convulsion take place they will be swept away—no matter which party conquers, if blind ignorance be paramount they must suffer. If, however, they at once go amongst the people—if they instruct—they may guide them. They may direct that power which none can destroy—they may obtain the willing co-operation of that power which alone can rescue them from the evils of an irresponsible government.[16]

Hume contributed two hundred pounds; Shuttleworth, Grote, and Warburton fifty pounds each; and William Ellis, Thomas Tooke, Edward Arnott, Charles Buller, Olinthus Gregory, W. J. Fox, and Perronet Thompson were among other supporters. The list of proposed contributors is a roll-call of distinguished radicals. In Place's circular letter, sent out in an attempt to raise sufficient capital by subscription, the project of a 'Penny Political and Moral Magazine' was stressed as a means of countering the heresies of the unstamped and the inefficiency of the regular press. It became apparent, however, after the debate in the House on 5 February, 1833, that ministers would not repeal the stamp taxes on newspapers, and the project came to an end, although eventually Roebuck determined to published his unstamped *Political Pamphlets*. Place held to the idea and, with a wonderful faith in the power of truth, was still hopeful of setting up such a society in 1836.

> It may be here observed that even the wildest notions entertained by the working people in respect to property are honestly entertained, religiously believed to be true, and such as when reduced to practice would be found advantageous to the whole community. Very few amongst them would entertain erroneous notions were both sides of every question fairly laid before them.[17]

Some sketches and explanations of the British Constitution appeared from individual writers and publishers, but they were concerned more with school children than adults.[18]   An instructive digression may, however, be made into the cognate field of history. History was undoubtedly a popular subject with English readers,[19] and, further, it was an important weapon on the intellectual side of political struggles. The appeal of the old radicals to the purity of the Saxon constitution is perhaps the first instance that comes to mind; and it is interesting that it was considered of enough weight to call out an answering periodical in 1817. This was *The Good Old Times; or, the Poor Man's History of England, from the Earliest Period Down to the Present Times*, which ran to twenty-eight weekly numbers, from 1 March to 13 September, priced at three halfpence and later at a penny. It was a warning against pretended friends, who cried up the past as an example to the present; and, while the usual sort of anti-Cobbett items appeared frequently, it was aimed primarily at showing how much greater was English liberty, and how much better English life in 1817, than in the 'good old times' of Alfred or

Elizabeth. The technique, as dishonest as the radical history was false, was to mix up a sort of history of abuses, based on extracts from Hume, with attacks on the present reformers, with the necessary parallels always implied if not, as was usually the case, made explicit. The other anti-radical use of history was, as indicated earlier, an appeal to patriotism, perhaps best illustrated in the historical sections of the *Plain Englishman*.

The radical idea was different, however. Samuel Smiles explained it in this way:

> How interesting, and how instructive, for instance, would be a course of readings or lectures on English History—a subject far too little known and studied even among what are called the educated classes of this country. I do not mean that history should be studied as a record of battles, conspiracies, and changes of dynasties,—or as a chronicle of the crimes of kings and their nobles, which it too often is; —but for the purpose of understanding the growth of the people—the development of their power—and their condition in past ages; at the same time that the moral sympathies are called forth in favour of the struggling masses, and the foul acts of rulers and governments, are held up to just censure and indignation.[20]

In short, how was the present state of society reached? The Chartists had their answers, which are lineally connected with the historical arguments advanced by the levellers in the civil wars; in this view Norman expropriation and the rapacity of aristocracy in general are perhaps the major themes. But historical argument—history as process—could be used as well to prove the necessity of the present disposition of society and the need for harmony among classes. John Wade's *History of the Middle and Working Classes* provides an historical sketch as introductory to an exposition of the principles of political economy, and perhaps no clearer example could be found than a plan advanced by an enthusiastic educator whose work is of the highest importance in this study.

In 1844 Harriet Martineau, her reputation assured by the political economy tales and the books on America, was working

with Seymour Tremenheere on a project for a periodical for
the miners of the northern coal-fields, to combat the influence
of the miners' own paper, a project which will be examined
more closely in a subsequent chapter. In the course of her
thinking about the plans, it struck her that nothing was being
done to instruct anyone in his duty as a member of society.
Reflecting the necessity of informal education, she remarked
in a letter to Tremenheere that no systematic plan of instruction
in such matters could be expected for a long time, but that a
humble beginning might be made.

Suppose I were to go back as far in the history of England,
as we have clear and procurable records of the modes of
life of our middle and working classes, and make stories,
presenting the aspects and probably incidents of their lives,
—which would show their relation to government and
the aristocracy, their position as members of Society—etc.
Are you aware how Ivanhoe is devoured by middling
people, for the sake of the Saxon modes of living represented
therein? From that time down to the present, the series
might extend, representing the function of every class,
profession or ruling influence of any kind,—the decline of
some orders and the rise of others,—the progress of civilization and *comfort* for all, and the essential need that every
class has of every other, etc., etc.—I seem to see how in
tales as plain as Red Ridinghood, and without a page of
preachment or exposition, a knowledge might be conveyed,
sound as far as it goes, of the British Constitution, in its
philosophy and its history—*Then with what power might we
address these readers, thus prepared, on the subjects on which they
are now so misled!* I could, but I need not enlarge on this.
I am persuaded that the idea is a good one. I am persuaded
that we shall reach our objects soonest by beginning so far
back.—By the time I come down to a Pit story and Wages,
the readers will have seen that their order is not, and never
has been, an *outcast* order, and many other truths which
we might now preach to them in vain.—I would write the
Tales as plainly as possible, and with a view,—not to poor
people, children, etc., but to the subjects themselves, as the
successive pictures pass before me.

She was certain that, if the books were done gratuitously and a circulation guaranteed, Knight would provide them with his organization for cheap paper, printing, and distribution. The plan came to nothing, though it seems highly probable that the largely historical *Forest and Game Law Tales*, which she wrote at the request of Bright in his anti-game-law (and incidentally anti-corn-law) campaign in 1845, were based on material worked over for this project.[21]

Tremenheere too made a contribution to political education by publishing in 1852 a little book called *The Political Experience of the Ancients, in Its Bearing upon Modern Times*, a digest of relevant parts of Aristotle, Polybius, and Cicero. As Plato's *Republic* is dismissed as impractical and the source of many doctrines of modern socialism and communism, these three authors 'embody nearly the whole of the "ancient wisdom" on the subject of constitutional government.' The net result is a paean of praise for mixed government, with the middle class predominant and the suffrage extended only so far as compatible with safety; and he is also careful to demonstrate the non-existence of true liberty under democracies and the maleficent influence of demagogues.

Books and projects like these were, however, neither common, nor publicized, nor apparently very successful. Politics, it seemed, was far too delicate and dangerous a subject. Yet one field of political instruction was exploited by these 'informal' educators, and it is important to inquire how and why this exception was not only admitted but widely advocated by middle class opinion. Political economy was their peculiar creed.

In the next three chapters it will appear how this powerful doctrine was employed in responses to the threat and opportunity found in a literate working class in three areas of tension, supplanting or mixing with the older approach. It is impossible in a study of this size devoted especially to 'crisis literature' to take up in any detail the fascinating history of the rapid spread of political economy as a cardinal article of middle class faith and of the many attempts to force a knowledge and conviction of this faith upon the working classes—a study of which I hope shortly to publish. But it is important to note in passing something of the hold which political economy took and to enquire precisely what was meant by it.

As a body virtually of revealed doctrine, political economy took final shape only after Malthus and Ricardo had made their original and striking additions to the work of Adam Smith. But even during its development, the ideas of the new science made rapid progress among the intelligentsia and some of the governing classes, as is witnessed by the Eden Treaty of 1786, the repeal of the apprenticeship statutes in 1813, the refusal on several occasions to enact protective industrial legislation, and the progressive freeing of trade begun under Tory auspices, following the Petition of the Merchants of London in 1820. The great work of popularization, however, began only in the twenties, with the publication of James Mill's *Elements*, McCulloch's *Principles*, and other similar outlines. The *Edinburgh* and *Westminster* were active propagandists ; professorships were set up in the universities and filled with the most distinguished exponents of the science whose own studies contributed to the refinement and further development of the subject; and Mrs. Marcet, early in the field, was only one of many writers who turned out elementary expositions suitable for the use of children and schools.

It was not simply the work of astute writers with a missionary faith that brought about the rapid acceptance of the new teaching; the doctrine itself was powerful and persuasive, or seemed so to ordinary minds adapting the work of serious thinkers to less scrupulous and objective needs in politics or business. In the first place, political economy was put forward as a science and accepted as such, often with the implication that it was as completely established and as unchangeable as the conclusions of Newton. More important, it rationalized a position which now can be seen to have been temporary, but which at the time seemed on the edge of a permanency which needed only a little more time and intelligence to be assured. Political economy could explain the triumph of British industry in its rapid assumption of economic supremacy over the rest of the world. It justified as well the claims to political superiority which the middle class advanced. As a Sorelian myth, the idea of laissez-faire was most impressive; class interest was unified around a theory which was continually violated in practice. And it offered a millenial future. It displayed the natural laws by which the economy and society operated. By pointing to violations of these laws, one could account for serious social difficulties; by advocating and teaching submission to the laws, one could prepare a golden age. In an expanding economy, with such a hope, one could easily overlook the pessimistic implications of a writer like Ricardo, whose picture of the future capitalist state was anything but encouraging.

As the science filtered down to the level of the ordinary business man, or as it appeared in the popularizers who wrote for the working classes, it became simpler, clearer, stronger, and less applicable. In this form it contains perhaps six principal points, far removed from the complexity of the founders, and probably the more potent for that. (1) A mechanistic 'Newtonian' view of economics, without human or social dimensions, and with a full complement of abstractions like 'labour,' 'capital,' 'free contract,' and so on. (2) A supreme concern with problems of production, and as a corollary the absolute benefit of machinery, notwithstanding any temporary distress caused by its introduction. (3) The canon of freedom—freedom of trade, freedom from government interference, and, above all for the working class audience, freedom of the labour market, with particular reference to the restrictive effect of trades unions. (4) The Malthusian theory of population in its simplest form: population tends to outrun subsistence, the former increasing geometrically, the latter arithmetically; from this follows the necessity of the limitation of numbers, by moral restraint, birth control, or emigration. (5) Stemming from Malthusian teaching was the theory of the wages fund— the so-called 'iron law'— in its crudest form, that there was a fund, fixed in amount, out of which wages were paid, and that the wage level varied as the proportion of this fund (and so of capital) and the supply of labour. (6) Finally, as both basic assumption and final deduction, the proposition that the interests of the working classes and of the middle classes were the same—the forwarding by all possible means of the interests and increase of capital, with the middle classes as the suppliers of the all-important capital in control of economic development and society. *142014*

It was a perpetual worry that propositions so self-evident as these did not carry conviction to the working classes and their allies. Many devout and benevolent persons in the upper classes, like Michael Sadler, refused to accept them, and worse were renegades like Hodgskin and Thompson who worked from the same or similar assumptions to radically different conclusions, anarchist or socialist. The working class press gave no quarter to the popular conceptions of political economy, and they did not carry on their attack in ignorance. Working class writers emphasized the origin of value in labour and asked the obvious question why the producers of value should turn over their creation to the capitalist. They objected to the use of cheapness rather than happiness as a criterion. They struck out at a system which preferred competition to co-operation and which persisted in regarding human beings as soulless instruments in a great machine. Further, working class leaders had their own doctrines to put forward in this period, as economic solutions Owenism and its variants, as political solutions real reform or the Charter. And they too propagated their faith.

There was then a contest for the minds of the reflecting and active parts of the working class. On one side were the working class press and the socialist and co-operative movements; on the other were the publicists and educators of the middle classes, like the Chamberses, Knight, McCulloch, Wade, Place, Mrs. Marcet, and Harriet Martineau. The conversions to political economy were few, but the socialists and co-operators did not win because of any innate superiority of their teachings or even of their technique. Indeed, when it suited their convenience, trade union leaders could accept some of the doctrines of the political economists. Their strength was that they continued to recognize the human needs and desires of the workers and the sources of their protests, while the advocates of political economy could never defend themselves satisfactorily against charges of hypocrisy. To claim the obedience due a science was not enough; it was hard to believe that providence had really ordained a system which created so ugly and degrading a civilization as the new industrialism, which the defenders could not explain away. John Ruskin surely found more readers among working men than did Harriet Martineau.

In the doctrines of political economy and their social implications lay probably the most clear-cut intellectual issue between the two classes. Working men, whose inferiority those doctrines proclaimed, could not accept them; the middle classes, whose supremacy they rationalized, had to get them accepted. And as a field for political instruction made essential by social tensions, they seemed not only necessary but safe. McCulloch makes this analysis clear, while underlining the reason advanced earlier for general unwillingness to take up the larger subject.

The sciences of Politics and of Political Economy are, therefore, sufficiently distinct. The politician examines the principles on which government is founded; he endeavours to determine in whose hands the supreme authority may be most advantageously placed; and unfolds the reciprocal duties and obligations of the governing and governed portions of society. The political economist does not take so high a flight. It is not of the constitution of the government, but of its ACTS only, that he is called upon to judge. . . . But he does this without inquiring into the constitution of the government by which these measures have been adopted. The circumstance of their having emanated from the privy council of an arbitrary monarch, or the representative assembly of a free state, though in other respects of supreme importance, cannot affect the immutable principles by which the economist is to form his opinion upon them.[22]

But political economy was not entirely an evasion. The segment was a science; the totality an art. The part was immutable; the whole perhaps open to question and overthrow. Political economy could be demonstrated from facts and statistics and so impressed on the rational mind of every man not utterly lost to prejudice and passion; politics could only be argued from disputable premises of history and fear. Might not conviction in one lead to acceptance in the other?

Three sources of tension in the thirties and forties—the agricultural disturbances of 1830-31, the poor law agitation, and trade unionism—provide particularly good opportunities to study the interplay of approaches to the working class reader, to observe the new machinery in operation, and to test the advocacy of the increasingly confident beliefs of a triumphant middle class. They are certainly not the only crises in which an appeal to the working class reader played a part;

but, for a selective study, they are clearly the best. Emigration propaganda is related to Malthusianism, but more closely to imperial developments. The struggle for factory legislation has left little controversy at this level in print. The reform struggle of 1830-32 found working class and middle class in considerable agreement, and the opposition pamphlets of unreconstructed tories are uninteresting and hardly even amusing. From Chartism one might expect much, but opposition to Chartism as such is not easy to find, outside of a few old-fashioned tracts and sermons. Perhaps indeed we are wrong to speak of a Chartist movement; perhaps Chartism was more an attitude than a movement, an attitude which found certain concrete outlets at particular times, and with two of these—poor law agitation and trade unionism—this study is very deeply concerned.

CHAPTER V

AGRICULTURAL DISTURBANCES
AND MACHINERY

At the end of 1830 occurred in the rural districts of the South of England what the Hammonds have called the last labourers' revolt, generally spontaneous outbreaks by miserable and half-starved country people resolved to submit no longer. Wages were incredibly low, six and seven shillings a week in southern counties, and supplemented out of poor rates, a system which penalized the independent worker by giving the advantage to his less provident or more unfortunate fellows, and which encouraged the growth of population by payments increasing with the number of children, legitimate or not. Such labour as was available to roundsmen and parish help was degrading. The diet of the rural poor had deteriorated. And working class memories are long and, like any memory, prone to idealization.

The disturbances began in Kent during the summer and spread rapidly through the county, spilling over into Sussex and Surrey in September. In mid-November, the infection spread to Berkshire, Hampshire, and Wiltshire. By December the disturbed area included Dorset, Gloucestershire, Bucking-hamshire, and Bedfordshire; alarming developments were taking place in East Anglia, while the Midlands were expected to break out at any moment, and fires were not unknown even in the North. Suddenly, by the end of December the trouble was over.

The early contagion had been helped on by a considerable show of sympathy from other classes, but fear of the seemingly general nature of the threatened insurrection soon put aside any benevolent inclinations and stiffened the pliant. Bargaining stopped, meetings were forbidden, wholesale arrests were made, gaols were filled, and special commissions were sent to the most seriously disturbed counties to look after the adminis-tration of justice while lesser areas were left to the no less sweeping scrutiny of regular assizes. The details of this savage legal repression do not belong here; the Hammonds provide them. Certainly it was that repression which broke the back of the movement; but there is one aspect of the counter-attack which the Hammonds overlooked or did not think of sufficient importance. It was of little importance in pacifying the rural districts; but it is a phenomenon of considerable importance in a study of the working class reader. This disturbance, like earlier disturbances, was to be written down.

Although some persons were willing to acknowledge deep distress as the real cause, it suited others, uneasy and suspicious, to seek some sort of malicious agency. Credit was lent to these suspicions by the simultaneous appearance throughout the country, even in the North, of letters signed by 'Captain Swing.' Agitators were reported travelling about the country in gigs and post chaises,[1] stirring up contented labourers, leading them to distrust their superiors, and encouraging them to incendiarism and machine-breaking. Sometimes they were foreign agitators, sometimes they were native; Cobbett was a particularly popular choice.

The press was a constant target. Certainly the radical press had some influence; it was read in groups or in public houses, in country and in town. For example, Joseph and Robert Mason transported for life at Winchester for offences growing out of the Hampshire troubles, regularly took in the *Political Register* and read it to a group of villagers.[2] Yet the press could hardly have played any really important role in country districts. Illiteracy was perhaps at its worst in the rural areas of southern England; and even the poor who could read a little (and there were some) were probably much too hard put to it to keep body and soul together, to spend even a penny or two on a paper. Frederic Hill, writing in 1836, noted that many attributed the disturbances to 'the excitement of political writing'; but such a position, he insisted, was in direct opposition to fact, an opinion with which Edwin Chadwick said that the best-informed persons agreed.[3]

Less well-informed minds did not maintain so reasonable a position; agency was the order of the day in their thinking. A land-agent and surveyor seemed to have no doubt that the disturbance arose 'from delusion among the peasantry, and attempts to inflame their minds, rather than from press of actual distress.'[4] A deeper plot was seen by Lord Wilton, who reportedly laid the estrangement of the lower orders from their superiors to 'the march of education, to the malign nastiness of the schoolmaster, to the spurious morality of the present day, and the dangerous influence of Mr. Henry, now Lord Brougham, and cheap libraries.'[5]

The most remarkable evidence on the point comes from the report of the Poor Law Commission in 1834. Of some 540 answers attempted to an item in a questionnaire asking to what the rioting and burnings of 1830 were to be ascribed, eighty-seven indicated the press as a sole or contributory cause.[6] This is a considerable number, made important by its reflection of local upper-class opinion, for the correspondents were clergymen, church-wardens, overseers, and magistrates. Very frequently they linked up seditious papers with the beer houses, which are certainly raised to the status of a major cause of the trouble by the answers. The beer houses, which multiplied rapidly after the act of 1830 made it easier to set up in the business, were to be found in remote places, away from the eyes of the magistrates; there labourers assembled and came into contact with bad men, bad literature, and bad ideas.[7] The confession of Thomas Goodman that he had been impelled to arson by a Cobbett lecture apparently made a deep impression, and the kind of impression that could not be erased by embarrassing questions about the manner in which that confession was obtained, or by Cobbett's subsequent acquittal.[8] Accusation always sinks deeper than absolution.

To some, however, reading and the press presented an opportunity, and, in view of the apparent success of radical propaganda, an opportunity which had to be seized at once. It has been pointed out that frequently in appeals to the working class reader the virtuous man who put down wickedness by his reasoning was a countryman. While disturbances in the towns were considered endemic by many, rural society was thought to be the essence of stability, and a threat in that quarter was a serious matter.

If lectures by radical agitators were printed and circulated with good effect, as was alleged, then why should not sermons against agitation be printed and circulated? They were. There is, for example, *An Address to the Labouring Population, on the Folly and Wickedness of Burning Agricultural Property*, published at Salisbury in 1831, and sold at sixpence or five shillings per dozen for distribution. It is the substance of a sermon preached in 1830 by G. F. Watkins, the curate of West Grimstead, Wilts. Rivington's, publishers *par excellence* to the Establishment, turned out numbers of sermons in cheap form in 1830 and 1831, and also caught an aspect of the situation in *A Short Address to Plain Sense on the Subject of Tithes*, which sold at a penny or fifty for three shillings and sixpence.

An Address to the Misguided Poor of the Disturbed Districts throughout the Kingdom was published by Rivington in 1830, and, so the title-page informs us, was sold also by booksellers in Norwich, Cambridge, and Yarmouth; that is, Rivington's served as a London outlet for material written and often printed in the provinces primarily for local circulation. A duodecimo pamphlet of forty pages—and so really too long for its purpose—it sold at sixpence or four shillings and sixpence per dozen, a price that certainly demanded, as did the title, distribution by the upper classes and the clergy. The author, the Reverend George Burges, urges the poor not to be set against the upper classes, or the government, or the clergy. Incendiarism is the worst crime of all: to destroy ricks is to destroy the maintenance of wives, children, orphans, aged, and widows; no gain can result, and exemplary punishment will be sure and swift. But his principal point seems to be a warning against demagogues and agitators. The nation is paying the price for permitting such publications as theirs to infest the land; for 'this refinement upon common villainy, this guilt doubled and trebled upon the soul' the country can thank in great measure the writings of Cobbett and Carlile. But, whatever change or revolution may come, the mass of mankind cannot be affected. ' "In the sweat of thy face shalt thou eat bread, till thou return unto the earth." God hath said it, and man, by no regulations of wisdom or government, can reverse it. . . .'

Similar sentiments, expressed perhaps less stringently, were offered to the poor even by the most liberal clergy. *A Letter to His Parishioners, on the Disturbances Which Have Lately Occurred* was published anonymously by 'a country pastor'; the author was Richard Whately, at the time of publication Professor of Political Economy at Oxford and soon to be Archbishop of Dublin. In this twelve-page tract, sold at twopence or one shilling and ninepence per dozen, he emphasizes the dangers of becoming the tools of wicked and designing men who seek to profit from the confusion which would result from the destruction of the institution of property. But factious leaders will fail, and those involved with them in their guilty acts will have much to answer for. Prudence is the better part, but a better restraint than worldly prudence is a strong sense of religion and a knowledge of Christianity. It is interesting that the Goldsmiths' Library contains an eight-page reprint of this letter from a print shop in Maidenhead; such republication was probably common and encouraged by local magistrates and clergy.[9]

Deserving of some attention for new points of emphasis is *A Word to the White Horse Men*, by a Berkshire magistrate, again published at Oxford for Rivington and Parker. His state of mind and the ineffectiveness of his approach are illustrated by the remarks he would use to one of the 'malicious cowards' who burn ricks, if such a person attempted to defend his crimes:

> *Did you ever see an Irishman?* Plenty, perhaps, and wished them at Jericho in harvest time. But mark; these poor fellows are driven over hither to escape starvation at home, in consequence of the state of things which you would produce here, if you dared. . . . Mark this; and, brute and savage as you may be, think at least of your own interests and food.

Could a greater ignorance of group loyalties be imagined than addressing in this manner the 'brave and honest men' of a village community? The significant feature of this pamphlet, however, is that the author emphasizes the necessity for moral restraint to limit population and the advantages of emigration, two favourite recommendations in the most advanced attempts to better the condition of the poor.

For more imaginative efforts, a natural gambit was provided by the mystery of Captain Swing, that personage whose name appeared in threatening letters throughout the disturbed districts, and whose card was often left behind at rick-burnings. Carlile published an 'autobiography' of Swing to show the intolerable suffering, from enclosure, at Peterloo, and in the traces of the parish cart, that drove poor honest Swing to his desperate acts.[10] There were at least two similar lives on the other side. One published by Effingham Wilson is called *A Short Account of the Life and Death of Swing, the Rick-Burner, Written by One Well Acquainted with Him*; it carries a woodcut and contains twenty-six pages. Its price of twopence undercut Carlile's price, but the title-page also bore a phrase which did not appear on Carlile's *Swing*: it was sold at one shilling and sixpence per dozen, to facilitate its free distribution. This 'life' sets out to refute the 'facts' of Carlile's account, and shows Swing as a careless, gin-drinking farmer, who fell under the influence of bad advisers. After an affecting last interview in Swing's cell, a peroration urges the reader to beware of 'infamous wretches' who care only for the poor as tools for their own horrible designs.

There is also *The Genuine Life of Mr. Francis Swing*, sold at twopence, under the imprint of W. Joy, St. Paul's Church Yard, and B. Hughes, St. Martin's-le-Grand. The date is 1831. Here poor Francis and his brother John are led astray by a radical missionary and tempted by a spectre to sell their souls to the devil. The doomed Swing is condemned to 'wander about the country in his gig,' sending threatening letters and burning down farmers' ricks. John on his deathbed cautions Francis against the Rotunda, where he had learned to despise the laws of God and man. ' "Oh, Francis! Francis! avoid that hell as you value your eternal soul!" "If by that hell you mean the Rotunda meetings, I must confess that I am a regular attendant there." My brother groaned twice deeply. "Then farewell every hope!" he said. . . .'

Tales were a favourite device. One by the Rev. I. E. N. Molesworth, *The Rick-Burners, a Tale for the Present Times*, of sixteen pages and priced at fourpence, was published at Canterbury in 1830 and went through at least three editions before the end of the year. *To Rioters and Incendiaries: a Letter Containing the Last Advice of a Rioter to Two of His Former Associates*, published by Hatchard in 1830, is really a little tale presumably put down by the parish minister, conveying for the dying man a proper tone of repentance after episodes of rioting and his wounding; but, if that were not enough, there is appended a list of the penalties to which rioters were exposed.

Machine-Breaking, and the Changes Occasioned by It in the Village of Turvey Down, published at Oxford and sold by Parker and Rivington, is a good example of the pat view. A naval officer had stopped to visit a college friend, the vicar of the pleasant village of Turvey Down. But when the officer returned a year later, the farm was laid low and deserted; the manor house was empty and its lawns overgrown; drunks staggered out of a beer house. The vicar sadly related to his friend how some lawless persons had aided rioting against harsh farmers in nearby Swingfield, and then had turned on the benevolent Lady Bonnington, demanding lower rents and tithes. The farmer's machines and barns were the next objects of their fury. He was ruined completely, and Lady Bonnington determined henceforth to live wholly in London. The two removals greatly lessened employment, the price of bread rose—the burned ricks alone could have fed the parish for two years— and the village of Turvey Down, once among the happiest, was now among the most wretched in England. And it had happened in the beer house: 'one or two notoriously disaffected men from a neighbouring village were often there, sometimes descanting upon the hardships and oppression of the poor, sometimes reading aloud inflammatory papers;—always heaping full measure of abuse upon the clergy, and sometimes in a sly underhand manner attacking religion itself.'

As always, dialogues were to be found. There is *A Dialogue on Rick-Burning, Rioting, etc. between Squire Wilson, Hughes, His Steward, Thomas, the Bailiff, and Harry Brown, a Labourer*, published by Rivington's and sold at threepence or half a crown for a dozen, and followed in 1831 by a second dialogue. Of particular interest in this genre is another effort by Whately, *Village Conversations in Hard Times*, published in two parts, early in 1831. It represents the conversation of Owen, a village schoolmaster, with Richard Ewell, a farm-labourer out of work because of the burnings, and John Latham, who was among the mob responsible. Owen meets all the objections raised by Latham or Mr. Black, a small tradesman turned agitator. The follies of destroying machinery, of equal division of property, of ascribing low wages to high rents and tithes are all demonstrated. Though Owen passes over in a rather unsatisfactory manner the objection that the upper classes may be blinded by their own interests, he makes it very clear that, among the savages, where all are equal, all are poor; and that the apostles were poor men who believed in the distinction between rich and poor and in the virtues of submission. The sad state of the lower classes is due to the growth of population and the lack of food to feed them. There speaks the political economist, and one of the political economist's cures—emigration—takes up the entire second part of sixty pages. A twenty-three page penny pamphlet put out by the active anti-reform publishers, Roake and Varty, in London, *A Plain Statement with Respect to Wages, Addressed Chiefly to Agricultural Labourers*, bears a heavy burden of political economy—chiefly the wages fund and the benefits of machinery—and reached a second edition. The new science also penetrated *A Country Rector's Address to His Parishioners, at the Close of the Twenty-fifth Year of His Residence among Them, with Reference to the Disturbed State of the Times*, by the Rev. E. Stanley, of Alderley, Cheshire, interesting as an illustration of how far the disturbances spread. It was printed in Macclesfield in 1830, was sold by Hatchard and Rivington in London, and reached a third edition by the next year.

Perhaps this small catalogue might best be closed by quoting the last exchanges of a dialogue, which must express very well the results that authors hoped might flow from their little books. *A Few Words in a Country Village*, published in Dorking at fourpence or three shillings and sixpence per dozen, is directed largely to the importance to the community of the spending of the wealthy. Then:

> *Blacksmith.*—I say neighbour, squire talks very sensible and well: and what a shame it is they should print such lying stories. I shall go and burn the little paper, and I wish I could meet the fellow who wrote it, I would teach him not to make a joke of me again.
>
> *Tailor.*—Aye, squire did not tell us so, but I know well enough that he spends more money himself among us in the parish, than his land brings him in, for his grandfather was

a Banker in London, and left him a large fortune, which he lives up to here.

Blacksmith.—It is very odd: I cannot make out how it is; but when I sit by myself, I grow more and more certain that we want some radical reform, but whenever I speak about it to any one who understands these things, I get convinced that we do not, and that it would do a great deal of harm: now I cannot make that out.

Labourer.—No more could I, till I happened upon the thirty-eighth chapter of Ecclesiasticus, and read from the twenty-fourth verse to the end, and then I found the reason, and that when squire can make ironwork like you, and clothes like you, or plough like us, we shall each probably be as able to be a parliament-man as he is. Every one to his own trade.

All.—Good evening.

So the good work went on. But Francis Place, who knew his working men, raised a disturbing question:

> Much has been said of the efficacy of talking and writing to the husbandry labourers; but these at present would be utterly useless, as to any immediate effects to be produced on them. They should long since have been taught, it is too late to expect immediate good consequences from talking to men circumstanced as they are; their object is an increase of wages, and this to them, has become past, present, and future; they carry their reasoning no further. Talk to one of these men with the half-crown in his fist which he has received for his day's labour; tell him of the mischief of burning stacks and extorting wages; he knows the farmer cannot pay, and the chances are ten to one, that he will show you the consequence of his conduct, by exhibiting the money, and reply to your arguments by laughing in your face.[11]

A writer in the *Westminster Review* commented also on the futility of the propaganda effort among an excited or illiterate working class, and urged the benefits of regular channels of communication over occasional addresses of the type examined here.[12] It was to be many years, however, before the newspaper penetrated the country districts in any force. In 1851, W. E.

Hickson, educational reformer and editor of the *Westminster*, expressed an opinion that agricultural labourers should read more about rick-burning.

> They meet at a beershop, for instance, to discuss the subjects of their grievances; some one perhaps expresses a strong opinion about some farmer having refused to give a certain rate of wages. One says, 'I wish somebody would burn down his ricks for him next week'; and some one of the party there does it. Now if they could read a paper containing an account about rick-burnings, the paper would perhaps inform them that they would do the farmer, after all, no mischief, because his stacks were insured; readers are not rioters; readers are not rick-burners.[13]

*

So far, this chapter has been concerned with appeals to working class readers which, in several forms and over a wide area, represent reactions to the general problem of agricultural disturbance on the part of magistrates and clergy. Except for Whately, who belongs in a sense to both worlds, the important middle class leaders in popular education have not appeared. Now two or three examples of their publications must be discussed. These people were also disturbed by the rural troubles, and their efforts will throw a good deal of light on distribution, problems, and reactions. But first something must be said about the immediate aspect of the problem on which they seized, for at this point the labourers' revolt of 1830 merges with a wider pattern of industrial discontent.

Threshing machines suffered badly in 1830, and often, for one reason or another, with the connivance of the farmers, who stood by quietly while the machines were smashed. It is understandable that machines designed to replace human labour should be attacked, when so many workers were starving for want of employment. Rick-burning was a form of revenge, but a senseless waste; machine-breaking too might be primarily for revenge, but it was more sensible—at least it was a material and actual enemy under attack, however futile the attack might be in the long run; and some comfort could be derived from that. Replaced labour has always hated replacing machines. Stockingers broke frames in the sixteenth century, so that legislation was necessary to protect the owners of the machines; and machine-breaking recurred at all periods of industrial strife, which were usually periods of hard times and unemployment. The Luddite disturbance of 1811-13 had attacked the masters primarily through attacking machines, and King Ludd's name was left behind, after the job was done, as Captain Swing's was left beside the blazing ricks of 1830.

The cures advocated by humanitarians, socialists, and the working class press, like taxing machinery or common ownership, were anathema to the political economists and their less thoughtful adherents, who by this time were growing very numerous indeed. With their powerful belief in progress went a tremendous fascination with the machine, which was the Word made iron. The remarkable increase in output and the lowering of prices of machine-produced material were sufficient proofs of its benefits. Any attempt to limit the introduction of machines, or to handicap their use once installed, was only to deliver the nation into the hands of foreign competitors. It was usually admitted that the introduction of a machine might cause some temporary inconvenience to the workers it replaced, but that was a minor matter in the face of the improvement of the general welfare which would result. It was vital to get this idea accepted.

The first tale which the young Harriet Martineau wrote on a current topic dealt with machine-breaking. *The Rioters: or a Tale of Bad Times* appeared in 1827, five years before the political economy series, and, as she says, before she knew precisely what political economy was. The newspaper taken in her family in Norwich suggested the plot for the tale, which was published by Houlston in Wellington. It is the narration of a business man, who came to Manchester in time of riot, where he encountered a poor weaver's family. The sons were sentenced for rioting, but the gentleman's explanations of the necessity of machinery to undersell foreign competitors, of the inevitability of fluctuation, and of the temporary nature of the distress restrained the father from further participation in the troubles. Thanks to the good offices of the traveller, the family was set on its way to modest prosperity. The story bears little trace of the science of political economy as it appears later in her series devoted to that subject; there is no mention of a redundant population or of the wages fund. Rather, starting from the suggestion in the newspaper, she must have drawn on her own experience and the experience and conversation of her family and their friends. The religious strain is slight, but sympathy with the distress that leads to rash acts is strong. Perhaps most significant is the faith in education which pervades all her works for the labouring classes: 'It is no fault of the government that your boys were not fully aware what they were doing. Every man ought to know, and in time every man will, I hope, know how he stands in relation to the government, and how important it is to his own security, and the good of society, that he should strictly observe the laws, whether he understands them all or not.' In the political economy series of 1832-34 the doctrine of machinery receives a much fuller statement in the second tale, *The Hill and the Valley*; again machine-breaking, now significantly as the result of an accident in which a careless boy was killed, drives industry and new prosperity from the valley.

The outbreaks of 1830 brought the Society for the Diffusion of Useful Knowledge into activity; hitherto its publications had been almost entirely confined to scientific and entertaining matters, and social and political projects had come to nothing. Here, however, was very grave necessity. So Brougham asked for permission to reprint Cobbett's 'Letter to the Luddites,' from the *Political Register* of 30 November, 1816. Negotiations fell through, for present purposes most instructively. Cobbett, in his 'Letter,' after an able and strong defence of the use of machinery, moved on to examine the reasons for distress, if machinery was not responsible ; of course, he found them in taxation, the debt, and the denial of reform. The permission to re-publish, which was given to Brougham, was accompanied by the condition that the whole must be published, and not extracts. When Brougham was subpoenaed to admit the embarrassing fact of the negotiations at Cobbett's trial in 1831, he explained that the condition made its publication by the Society impossible,

not on account of anything bad in the contents of any part of it, but that it contained matter which we did not deem consistent with our usual course, not from anything criminal or improper. . . . Some observations on individuals or something of that kind which the Society could not publish.[14]

If the whiggish Society dared not cope with unabridged Cobbett, it had to do something, and the hurried result was *An Address to the Labourers, on the Subject of Destroying Machinery*, an eight-page octavo pamphlet which appeared early in December, priced at a penny, with a reduction for quantity. It sets out to show that a threshing machine is only a more efficient tool. Would not a carpenter, of whom a labourer demanded that he give up his best tools, think the labourer mad? The destruction of machines will not cure the evils complained of, but only increase them by raising the price of corn; and combined with the worse crime of burning, it must spread famine. The excess of labour in relation to the means of employment is the responsibility of previous generations, but the remedy is not to be found in employing two men to do work better done by one. The best relief lies in the desire of landlord and tenant to pay a sufficient wage to those employed, and to support and comfort those who are out of work. 'An increase of trade, commerce, manufactures, as the Country prospers, will cause an increase in the growth of corn, to supply the food of those who labour in manufactories; fresh mouths to feed will require more food for their use, and take up the Labourers who are now unemployed in the fields.'

The Society's organization of local committees and high-pressure publishing enabled them to get out 20,000 copies in a few days, and a sale of 120,000 additional copies followed.[15] Reactions to the address were most favourable. A correspondent in Whitley requested on behalf of a local committee a thousand copies to be sent by coach as soon as possible. In Exeter a gentleman saw to the distribution of the addresses sent him in the principal workshops and public houses in the neighbourhood, while he also planned their insertion in one or more newspapers. He had received many applications for copies, he said, and, if the committee would send him as many as they wished distributed in Devon, he would see to it that they were sent to every public house in almost every town in the county. He also suggested another idea that had occurred

to him for effective distribution—the sending of a few copies
to each of the receivers of deposits for savings banks, of which
there were about a hundred and fifty in his area. Newspaper
and public house distribution was also relied on about Liverpool and in Cheshire.[16]

Apparently the addresses were sent out in packets of fifty,
and requests for more were common. T. W. Hill, of Hazel-
wood, Birmingham, the brother of the better known Rowland
and Matthew Davenport Hill, announced that he had put his
fifty copies into active, and, he hoped, effective circulation,
and promised to turn a further two hundred to good account.
On the same day his son wrote asking that fifty or a hundred
copies be sent to a schoolmaster in Worcestershire who would
see to their distribution in useful quarters in agricultural districts in that county. B. H. Malkin, professor of history in
the University of London, and his son were also active. The
younger man wrote to Coates of accounts indicating unrest in
Glamorganshire which might be met by the circulation of the
addresses; similarly a corner of Bedfordshire near Cambridgeshire and the area around Bury in Suffolk were disturbed.
He addressed notes to three gentlemen who he thought would
circulate copies of the address judiciously, and asked that the
usual number be sent, if official covers could be got. The elder
Malkin, resident in Cowbridge in Wales, wrote complaining
that the promised addresses had not arrived, and fearing that
they might have been mis-sent to Cambridge, a frequent error;
he included requests for small packets to other correspondents
in Wales. A further letter from the son indicated that his
father was receiving applications for more addresses, and could
perhaps dispose of a further one hundred, particularly at an
imminent meeting of landholders and farmers in the neighbourhood to petition for an alteration in tithe laws. He also
asked that one hundred be sent to Joseph Price, an engineer
and active Quaker, who would get them out among the
manufacturing labourers about Swansea. James Loch, writing
from Newcastle, requested a thousand copies in addition to
those already received which he had distributed in the lead
mining and other distant districts. 'In this neighbourhood
our labourers of all kinds are fully employed at fair wages,
and appear to be all satisfied and quiet—They are, however,

fond of reading, and as they have formerly been somewhat restless the Address may do good among them.' His bookseller hoped to circulate a good many by selling them at low prices, a scheme he believed more effective than giving them away.[17]

The Society's next contribution was on a larger scale; this was the celebrated *Results of Machinery, Namely, Cheap Production and Increased Employment Exhibited: Being an Address to the Working-Men of the United Kingdom*, written anonymously by Charles Knight and published as a volume of the series known as *The Working Man's Companion*. It was without doubt a bargain—216 pages, for a shilling sewed, or one shilling and threepence in cloth, or in six numbers at twopence each. The idea occurred to Knight early in December, when the panic had reached its peak. He remarked, in looking back, that it was unlikely that a 'sober and argumentative' little book, with no appeal to the passions, would save a single threshing machine; but 'no good seed is utterly thrown away, even if it fall at first upon a barren soil.' The enthusiastic reception which the book received is a token of the need that was felt for it, although Knight attributed part of the popularity to its having been ascribed, quite without foundation, to Brougham himself. For the Useful Knowledge Committee, Spring Rice, then chairman, told Knight, 'somewhat hyperbolically,' that it had done more good than a regiment of horse in any disturbed county. The *Athenaeum* called it more valuable than special commissions and other paraphernalia of repression, and hoped that 'every gentleman in the country [would] distribute his hundred—twenty shillings will give him 120.'[18]

The letters sent to the S.D.U.K. certainly do not contain so many requests for the *Results of Machinery* as for the smaller and cheaper address. Some there are, however: Malkin asked for several sets for friends in Wales and particularly for four dozen sets to a Mr. Charles Redwood, of Cowbridge. One of the Strutts, in Derbyshire, asked for twelve dozen copies in cloth at as large a discount as possible, to distribute at the lowest possible price. And a fulsome letter from a petty clerk in Bolton asked for copies to be used in his personal campaign to instruct the working classes.[19] It seems most probable that Mrs. Marcet was expressing as much a reality as a wish when,

in one of her simplest political economy tales, she made John
Hopkins say:

> I have learnt a good deal from talking with my landlord,
> who has a great knack at these things, and he gave me a little
> book, called 'The Working Man's Companion'; but small
> as it is, there's a world of knowledge in it. I found it rather
> hard at first; but he helped me on with it by an explanation
> now and then; and it's there I learnt all the good that comes
> of machinery, and the folly and wickedness of opposing it.[20]

Knight begins his volume by attempting to establish the
inevitability of machinery. The tone at the outset is one of
condescension; it could not avoid giving offence today, and
it is difficult to believe that it would not have caused an uncom-
fortable feeling then. He goes on to show what the book would
be like, if it had to be made by hand, and then proceeds to
illustrate the virtues of machinery in agriculture and mining.
Drawing on the observations he made during his northern
journey for the S.D.U.K. in 1828, he devotes the next one
hundred and fifty pages to descriptions of the uses of machinery
in various industrial processes. These portions of the book,
well-written and obviously interesting, represent nicely the
wonder which contemporaries felt in regarding their accom-
plishments. But, interest aside, he is open to the charge, which
was made subsequently, of belabouring the obvious. When
at length he returns to his argument, he points out the function
of capital in setting men to profitable work, and explains the
danger of a flight of capital from the tyranny of the mob.
His next point is to show that, in the event, machinery both
cheapens production, thereby increasing the benefit to the con-
sumer, and increases employment, through expanded and
cheaper production. Finally, he comes to the question of the
inevitable distress. It is not, he says, his province to enter into
the collective actions of society which might mitigate the
temporary evils which follow on improvement, although he
assures the reader that society cannot interfere to stop the
improvement itself; rather he sets himself to show what the
individual can do to help himself over the difficult period. His
recommendations to working men are two: first, to get knowledge, both of their capabilities and duties, and of such prac-

tical kinds as will enable them to shift their occupation readily, as the 'caprices of fashion' vary the demand for employment; the second is a justly famous passage urging the workers to imitate the farmer who can withhold his corn if the price in Mark Lane is too low.

> When there is too much labour in the market, and wages are too low, do not combine to raise the wages; do not combine with the vain hope of compelling the employer to pay more for labour than there are funds for the maintenance of labour; but go out of the market. . . . You have, in too many cases, nothing but your labour for your support. We say to you, get something else; acquire something to fall back upon. When there is a glut of labour go at once out of the market; become yourselves capitalists.

The faults of the little book are self-evident today. But what did contemporary critics think? The *Spectator* thought it an able 'palaver,' intelligible and amusing, and they looked for considerable good to come from the extensive circulation of the work. But they found it much too long for general perusal, and too elaborate; it could hardly penetrate to the agricultural labourers, who had been the principal offenders. The reviewer in the *Quarterly* pointed out that preaching the general advantage of machinery was not enough; too many cutting questions —for example, whether a comparative exemption from taxation did not give an unfair bounty to the employment of machinery, or whether owners were not being enriched at the workers' expense—were avoided. As for the recommendation to become capitalists, the reviewer thought it worthy of notice, 'if only for its singular infelicity.'[21]

A very able pamphlet was published by the journeyman bookbinders of London, whom Knight had accused of a dog-in-the-manger attitude towards a new beating machine. Utility and experience, not cheapness and *a priori* determination, are suggested as the criteria for introducing machinery. Particular objection was taken to Knight's urging labourers to 'become capitalists,' when the principle of cheap production denied the labourer the means of doing so.[22] And a similar view was expressed to a working class audience in Birmingham the next year. The recommendation was a species of mockery.

For the labourer the problem of machinery was one to be treated only in very concrete and very human terms, and not by doctrine and neat postulates.[23]

The crux of the matter could not be better put than it was by a writer in the *Spectator* in 1841; he referred to the very stubborn fact that

'there is a temporary evil occasioned by the introduction of a new machine, inasmuch as certain hands are immediately disemployed.' That is a fact which your thoroughpaced political economist can take as easily as a five-barred gate, while the plebeian hackney, the working-man, finds it stop him at the outset. The benefit to many—the advantage in the long run—the increase to the population in the towns of Leeds and Paisley—are things which he may know and admit, but they touch him not; whereas the fact that he, or some man he knows, was suddenly cut short in the employment of his life by a new machine, brings his study of political economy to a dead halt. . . .[24]

Machine-breaking died out; in industrial areas it had been declining since the terrible days of the Luddite affairs, and the agricultural breakings—which extended to foundries and factories in rural areas—were by a different group of workers. Perhaps they were learning through education in schools and pamphlets; more likely, they were learning through concerted action. The impact of England's industrial expansion was also a major cause of this change of view; despite the hardships of the forties, some workmen were prospering—particularly those who are called the aristocrats of labour—and there were great outlets for surplus labour in the colonies and the demands of the railroad builders.

There is no evidence to support a contention that the little publications were really useful. Two friends of the S.D.U.K. made disturbing comments. One thought the *Results of Machinery* well adapted to its object, but not to his purpose; neither this nor the shorter articles found their way to the lower classes, and, had they done so, the longest of them would not have been read, save by a comparatively few persons. A member writing from Reigate thought the book too good, because too elaborate and too long, and, despite its entertaining contents, 'unintelligible to the mass of the farming Labourers and common people, although among the Manufacturers it would be different. An abstract . . . or a few propositionss and short reasonings printed on a card or a quarter of a sheet and sold for a penny would be more likely to do good.'[25]

Finally, a correspondent of Place's, writing from Cottishall, Norfolk, 14 January, 1831, recounted his experience, which must be quoted in full:

The thing uppermost in my mind is that notwithstanding the quantity of light in this country there is a mass of ignorance which it will take generations to remove as it seems to me. Reading is cheap thanks to the society for the diffusion of knowledge, in a great degree. But some who are well off live amongst ignorant folks and will not read, our farmers and labourers in part will not in part cannot. I bought last week 6 copies of the society's penny address on the destruction of machinery and have been able to give away but two. When I read it I said this will not do for people unaccustomed to read, but I will try. I gave a copy to Ben B. and said read this Ben and tell me what you think of it and then give it to Will S. and Ben P. These are steady industrious men of good sense who can read and write decently. Well Ben, what do you think of it? 'Why, Sir, I can't exactly understand it but I can make out that the Book says the folks have a *wonderful malice* against threshing machines.' These were his words; of the reasoning he had no apprehension. Then W. S. what do you make of it? 'Why, Sir, I can't exactly satisfy my own mind.' Do you mean you don't understand it? 'Yes, Sir, I can't say I understand it.' What does your partner Ben say? 'Oh, Sir, Ben laughed amazingly.' Now Ben is a very grave fellow and what he found to laugh at I can't tell, but I know that reasoning on paper is to him gibberish and thus ridiculous. I gave another copy to a master bricklayer, a very shrewd man, but he has not found time for it, short as it is. I gave him also a most interesting little volume by the same society, 12mo, on machinery, 1/3. Though I live amongst labourers and farmers I can find no one yet to give more to. They have no political existence, nor will they till they get the use of their understanding.

Nine-tenths of these men would have signed against Catholic Emancipation, one told me when that was carried, he wished our rulers would read the prophets. 'Why, John,' said I, 'is there any thing there about Catholic Emancipation?' 'Oh, yes, Sir, I think it is laid down wonderfully plain in Habbakkuk.' So I gave him up, he could not read the penny address, but clearly understood what I could make nothing of. At a farmer's ordinary lately all at the table were against me on educating the poor; they attributed all the mischief to knowledge, I to ignorance. I find it like talking to the wind. Our labourers understand Cobbett but do not read him.[26]

The crisis of 1830-31 was solved by a savage repression; the Hammonds have demonstrated that. And, in considering the apparent deficiencies in distribution and the clear hostility of the audience towards the efforts discussed here, one must tend to agree with Francis Place in his doubts about the effectiveness of little books. Neither *ad hoc* argument nor long-term theory stood much chance of acceptance from a half-starved worker, faced with an acute and personal 'knife-and-fork question.'

CHAPTER VI

THE NEW POOR LAW

SOME of the tracts addressed to the poor during the French revolutionary period stressed the poor laws as one of the advantages enjoyed by the poor of England which might be destroyed by the implementation of French ideals or—by not inaccurate implication—by native reform. But the next few years pretty well finished off the tendency to laudation of the poor laws; and the man responsible for the change was, above all, Malthus, whose *Essay on Population* appeared in 1798, achieving an impact which the qualified later editions did not much modify. The poor laws were declared to be England's ruin, their abolition was proclaimed the safety of the state, and charity became a distinctly suspect virtue. One of the assistant commissioners of the celebrated enquiry of 1832-34 declared, in fact, that if a trustee of a charity for distributing doles misappropriated the funds to his own pleasure, or if a trustee of a foundlings' charity kept a mistress with the money, less immorality would be produced than by literal administration of the trust.[1]

Malthusianism was the most important, but far from the only theoretical impulse to the enactment of the notorious amending act in 1834.[2] Economically, that act owed much to the belief in a free market for labour, for the settlement laws were drastically altered. Politically, it reflected the bourgeois triumph, with popularly elected, property-holding rate-payers choosing guardians to replace patrician and irresponsible magistrates. Administratively, and even in terminology, it owed nearly everything to Jeremy Bentham and his bright young men: the workhouse test and 'less eligibility' were the keys to relief, and the crowd of inspectors and the trio of commissioners in Somerset House adumbrated the *Constitutional Code* and gave Lord Eldon a severe constitutional shock.[3]

The immediate stimuli and objects of the act were, on the sponsors' own showing, three. To evaluate their importance is difficult, for they were advanced, concealed, hinted at, denied, and acted upon variously as the situation demanded. The object which will appear most frequently in this chapter is that of raising the condition of the labouring classes from improvidence and degradation to independence. Undoubtedly many persons were concerned about the dreadful pass to which, since Speenhamland in 1795, some poor law administration had come, and which had made the beneficiaries of the laws into victims; but it seems unlikely that this factor alone could have brought action. Amendment was necessary to 'arrest the progress and ultimately to diminish the amount of the pressure on the owners of lands and houses.'[4] Rates had risen fabulously in the South, and a generation quite unprepared for redistribution of income were certainly unwilling to have it done in so unsubtle a fashion. The other important factor was the agricultural disturbance of 1830. The poor laws had been all along a system of social police, which had imperatively to be strengthened; the upper classes had long been worried, but they were at that moment very frightened. Malthus insisted that if

> the lower classes of people could be convinced that, by the laws of nature, independently of any particular institutions, except the great one of property, which is absolutely necessary in order to obtain any considerable produce, no person has any right on society for subsistence, if his labour will not purchase it, the greatest part of the mischievous declamation against the unjust institutions of society would fall powerless to the ground.[5]

After 1830, theory was strongly reinforced, even overwhelmed, by urgency.

The Royal Commission on the Poor Law, appointed in 1832, is a landmark in many ways. It set a pattern of enquiry; its recommendations were new and startling; and its members and supporters realized, as it had not been realized earlier, the importance of cultivating public opinion in favour of a proposed change. A writer in the *Quarterly* had long before urged the necessity of putting the poor law system to the public in

a popular intelligible form, for 'the knowledge thus disseminated would be an excellent preliminary to a measure never to
be lost sight of, the gradual abolition of some of those objectionable parts of the poor laws, which are equally condemned
by reason and experience, and by which no one is ultimately
more aggrieved than the operative workman himself.'[6] A mass
of pamphlets had helped to prepare the ground; and, as the
reports came in from the assistant commissioners, they were
condensed for a volume issued in 1833 containing the essence
of the evidence in something over four hundred octavo pages,
sold at four shillings.[7] The idea was Brougham's.

The distribution of the *Extracts* was followed in 1834 by
the publication of the report, which sold more copies, thought
Chadwick, than all the other state papers put together that had
been put before the public; he estimated that over twenty
thousand copies were circulated.[8] But official publications
were not enough. A majority of the newspapers, the *Times* at
their head, were against the government. Chadwick wrote to
Charles Knight in March, 1834, that the government would
have 'up-hill work' to carry the reform through, and would
need 'all direct and indirect aid that the press and good men
can give them.'[9]

Chadwick could hardly have appealed to a more active or
enthusiastic supporter of the proposals, or to one whose resources in popular publishing were greater. Knight's poor law
publication, on his own as well as through the S.D.U.K., is
quite phenomenal. In 1834, for example, he published a sort
of digest of the digest of evidence, in two parts, sketching the
operation of the law and the proposed remedies. The two
parts came to ninety-five pages in all, and sold at fourpence
for each section.[10] His *Companion to the Newspaper* devoted the
supplement of July, 1833, to the poor laws, providing an
historical introduction to the subject, a sketch of the advantages
of a poor law, and an outline of the provisions and defects in
the English system, the necessity for remedying which was
stressed; the article was based on the report of the Commission.
When the report was published, another article appeared in
the *Companion* for April, 1834, and another on the bill itself
in July.

The S.D.U.K., with both Brougham and Knight to urge it

on, and, on this subject, without apparent internal opposition, was active in the proselytizing. In 1832 had appeared *Hints for the Practical Administration of the Poor Laws*, a nineteen-page pamphlet, written by R. A. Slaney, and published as a part of the *Farmer's Series*. It was a purely administrative pamphlet, the principal recommendations for more effective operation within the old system being the adoption of paid overseers and select vestries under Sturges Bourne's Act, and the more general use of the poor house coupled with a cessation of the allowance system.

Perhaps the most celebrated and extensive propaganda effort for the reform was undertaken for the S.D.U.K. by Harriet Martineau at the request of Brougham. She was at the time still engaged on the political economy series and was somewhat reluctant to take on the added burden; but Brougham's arguments about the help her stories would give won her over. It was agreed that the series should be published by Charles Fox, publisher of the *Illustrations*, under the super-vision of the S.D.U.K. The price agreed upon was seventy-five pounds for each story on the day of publication, while Brougham himself promised to add another twenty-five to make up the hundred pounds he insisted was the proper price. The Society fulfilled its obligation promptly, but she never heard from her erratic sponsor, a fact which certainly did nothing to allay the strong hostility she developed towards him on other grounds, political and personal.[11] The first part of the first tale was submitted to the Committee in late February, 1833, and the second in July, although a long outline of the plan was sent in March. There was the usual delay in getting the proof through the Committee, and the worried author wrote to Coates emphasizing that 'this is not the sort of work which may as well come out at one time as another.'[12] The four tales finally appeared in late 1833 and early 1834.

She had already paid her respects to the poor laws in *Cousin Marshall* in the political economy tales; in the poor law tales, she set out to show two things—the evil turn to which matters had been brought by the operation of the old poor laws, and the great benefits which would flow from the adoption of the new proposals. It is to the former that the greatest amount of space is devoted. Abuse after abuse is shown, often quite graphically—the tremendous burden which an 'easy' parish laid on the farmer and the independent poor; the degradation of the pauper population and their susceptibility to agitation; the profiteering and conniving of officials; the inequalities of assessment on outworn valuations; the evils of the law of settlement; and so on. The remarkable second tale, *The Hamlets*, contains the major suggestions for reform—the workhouse test, the principle of less eligibility, the union of parishes, paid officers. One of the most significant and most violently attacked features of the new programme, the centralized administration, is, however, referred to only in passing in *The Town*, probably because it did not lend itself sufficiently well to illustration. The tales, as tales, are perhaps better than the average tale of the larger series, as their development is not hindered by the necessity of expounding doctrine, and the author could choose striking incidents from the great storehouse of the report and turn them to good account. An accurate reflection of the general operation of the poor laws they are not; nor, for that matter, are the Commissioners' reports. Both were drawn on certain preconceptions and a conviction of the necessity for action. Both set out to convince, to educate the public.

Harriet Martineau had misgivings. Her letters to W. J. Fox indicate that she was concerned lest she might be thought moving from one political group into another. In his review of the first tale in the *Monthly Repository*, Fox regretted that she allowed herself to be diverted to the new task, when the larger one remained unfinished, and warned that her association with the S.D.U.K. might make her 'a less efficient, because less trusted, national instructor.'[13] Perhaps the most eloquent comment on the success of the series is that Charles Fox lost £380 by the publication.[14]

The bill carried with no difficulty at all. Senior thought that no great measure had ever passed more easily, even triumphantly, opposed only by a few die-hard tories, a few ultra-radicals, profiteers, and sentimentalists.[15] Of course, it carried so easily because it fitted the interests of nearly everyone who was represented in Parliament. And the most remarkable thing about the propaganda mentioned so far is that it seems unmistakably to have been directed to those represented classes, to the very groups who really did not need it. The sponsors of the reform seem to have been much more worried by the *Times* than by Cobbett. Charles Knight wrote triumphantly that the bill had passed, despite the clamour against it, because the people no longer allowed their thinking to be done for them; they had not escaped the inoculation of political economy.[16] But it is very clear that a considerable proportion of the population had not only escaped the inoculation of political economy but had actively resisted it. Somehow, the publicists of poor law reform had forgotten the poor.

Francis Place wrote to Harriet Martineau early in 1834 that her *Parish* had done much, and that the octavo report would do much more, but that good on a large scale would depend on the act and the commissioners.[17] Perhaps that is as satisfactory an explanation as can be found for the mushrooming of the agitation against the new law after its passage. The working class press had been hammering away at the proposals long before they were put into effect; Oastler and his friends realized what was going to happen and tried to enlist help against it. But it was not until the law was actually put into operation, first in the South, later in the North, that the ordinary labourer came to realize, often through harsh experience, what it meant; and he was then quite ready to turn to his paper or to a speaker for a recital of poor-law atrocities, true or not.

Cobbett maintained that the object of the new law was to make the poor of England live on a coarser sort of food, to reduce them to the level of the Irish; and he repeated his charge again and again. Further it was 'a sort of *Austrian* project' to build up the executive and to abrogate local government—that was what 'a brace of bishops, a brace of lawyers, and two couple of newspaper reporters, or something of that sort, [were] capable of recommending, as the suitable treatment for the most unfortunate part of the working people of England.' His little comedy of 1831, called *Surplus Population*, was played with great success in rural areas in southern England. The *Poor Man's Guardian* pointed to outbreaks of incendiarism, not justifying but explaining them: the poor man could not respect property acquired through fraudulent laws and institutions. 'That Act, we repeat, must be repealed;

unless it be repealed, and quickly, too, half the produce of the country will be burned in the approaching winter.' Oastler, Stephens, Samuel Roberts, Robert Blakey, John Fielden, radicals, and church-and-king tories opposed the new law even to the point of violence. And Chartist leaders found opposition to the law a certain means of getting response even in politically lethargic areas.[18]

The press shared the agitation with the platform; and it would be impossible to list here the pamphlets and working class papers which carried on the fight. Nassau Senior, who in 1834 was certain of support from 'all the tenpounders and all the respectable mechanics,' from everyone capable of understanding reasoning, 'as the subject is not one of much difficulty . . .'[19] had changed his views seven years later. While the upper classes were little influenced by the press, he wrote, it was far different with the shopkeepers, artisans, and middle classes in the country; there newspapers were all-powerful, for little else was read, and even the shallowest writer was superior in knowledge to his reader, who was not equipped to detect his sophistries and falsehoods by reason of possessing no habit of reflection and study. Apparently the dimensions of the agitation had caused Senior to change his mind about the ease of convincing the public about the virtues of the new policy. Now he maintained that the principles of the act were neither obvious nor easy to understand.

> But to attack it is the easiest thing in the world. There is not a single portion of the whole measure on which an unscrupulous writer, addressing an ignorant or a prejudiced reader, could not pour out a column of unpremeditated invective.[20]

The immediate counter attack was to appeal to the working classes on the basis of facts and on the basis of their respectability. The first fact which had to be got across was a knowledge of precisely what the new procedure involved. Directly he heard of Chadwick's appointment as secretary to the new Commission, Place sat down and wrote a letter, urging a cheap publication of the act with explanations in non-technical language.

Make the whole bill plain and clear to all men, and it will go far towards making it work well. It will answer by anticipation those who are disposed to work hard to throw discredit upon it, but it must be done at once, be printed off hand—sold for a small sum—and it should be the same size as the 'Report,' etc. It will make a volume about half as thick as the report. I think this suggestion is of importance and hope you will not take too much time in thinking of it, but will set about it forthwith, that an announcement may be made, which while it will cause many enemies, and many fools to hold their vituperative tongues, will push aside a whole host of mischievous writers.[21]

The act was published, more or less officially, edited and supplied with explanatory notes and an index by John Tidd Pratt, a barrister who had helped to draw up the bill. The second edition, published in 1834 as well, was preceded by a preface 'containing a popular outline of the act' by Nassau Senior. Unlike the report, it was published in duodecimo, one hundred and forty pages for half a crown, certainly a vastly higher price than Place would have approved, although he reported that copies were given away. The Senior outline was also published separately. Handbooks and guides to relief were published, usually coupled with some sort of defence of the act; a number of examples of such publications will appear, more for the interest of the latter function than the former, but the persistence of the attempt to get across the bare facts of administrative procedure should be kept in mind.[22] The new law was also explained to the poor in lectures. Sir Francis Bond Head, an assistant commissioner, prepared an address to the labouring classes for delivery in his area in Kent; one James Acland appeared in Rochdale to empty benches and the scorn of the *Northern Star*; and Cobbett wondered if the lecturer at Norwich on the reform proposals was a member of Brougham's Useful Knowledge Society.[23]

Pamphleteering on the subject was widespread; the authors were poor law or parish officials or benevolent individuals convinced of the virtue of the new act, or, above all, parsons. In rural areas parsons were the natural publicists, and for the poor law they served much as they did in the disturbances of 1830, although their productions were likely to be more practical and less theological than in the earlier period. Scriptural authority was used, however. In a sermon preached and published in 1839, Francis Close, perpetual curate of Cheltenham and later Dean of Carlisle, chose to rely chiefly on the important appeal to the industrious workman as against his idle fellow, but he was also at pains to point out that the new system was not only expedient and beneficial, but 'that its general principles are based upon sound reasoning and scriptural truth. The advocates of universal almsgiving and unrestricted pauperism may search the Scriptures in vain for any divine authority for their system.'[24] So too Sidney Godolphin Osborn, then incumbent at Stoke Poges, subjoined to the little pamphlet he wrote for his parishioners a table listing five objects of the act with quotations from the Bible to buttress them. Called *A Word or Two about the New Poor Law*, it is a chatty little fourteen-page tract, printed in London in 1835 and sold at twopence or twelve shillings a hundred; it ran to at least eleven editions within a year. Clergymen could also preach political economy; at any rate, Thomas Spencer, uncle of Herbert Spencer, did so. In a few years, he said, it would seem incredible that men of intelligence could speak of political economy with contempt; and in his view the new poor law was honoured rather than discredited by sharing the reproach against 'this noble science.'[25]

The Rev. T. Garnier, jun., fellow of All Souls and curate of a Hampshire parish, published *Plain Remarks upon the New Poor Law Amendment Act, More Particularly Addressed to the Labouring Classes* at Winchester in 1835, coupling as justification for the act the degradation of the labourers he was addressing and the pressure of rates on their employers. It will be recalled that Senior had cited these two reasons in his memorandum for Brougham; but most of the writers for the poor preferred to overlook the argument about the rates and to concentrate on the role of the new act in raising the condition of the degraded labourer. One, for example, writing for Kentish labourers, maintained that he would never have upheld the law, were it only to save money; the system was changed, not because it was expensive, but because it plunged labourers into pauperism. With charity so widely offered, 'is it fair that we should be accused, is it just or right that we should be suspected, of an intention to grind and oppress the poor for the purpose of saving our money?' He concluded on a note that reflected another worry of the time, urging the labourers not to look to 'deceitful schemes of unions and secret societies,' which began in folly and ended in disappointment.[26]

Proof of the benevolent intentions of the act was to be had from reports of its actual operation. The British chaplain at Rotterdam, lately vicar of Little Horwood, Bucks, said as much.

> A publication of facts on the real operation of the *Poor Law Amendment Act*, accompanied by sound and calm reasoning, cannot fail to dispel much of the present misapprehension. All that the supporters of this legislative provision require of those who oppose it, is a fair hearing, and that credit should be given them for acting from honest and good intentions.[27]

A good example of an effort of this kind is provided by the Buckingham Union. Apparently the labouring population of the union refused to believe favourable accounts reported to them from paupers sent from different parts of the country into the manufacturing districts and preferred to listen to unfavourable reports from 'one or two idle and disaffected persons who have returned from Lancashire.' In consequence, the guardians chose two labourers to be sent, suitably accompanied, to see for themselves. They reported to the assistant commissioner who supplied them with information. Rates of wages and prices were duly set down in a little pamphlet. All the Bucks emigrants in Stalybridge reported, with an exception or two, good wages, pleasant work, and no desire to return. One of the visitors stayed on at twelve shillings a week; the other was offered the same, but his cicerone wanted him to return to lend credence to the report. The pamphlet ends with a letter from one of the emigrants.[28]

John Leslie, vestryman and governor and director of poor in the model parish of St. George, Hanover Square, was among the most active of propagandists. His *Practical Illustration of the Principles upon Which the Poor Law Amendment Act Is Founded*, based on the procedure in his parish, was published in 1835 and ran to at least fifteen editions. Six thousand copies were printed and distributed to ratepayers at the expense of fifty-eight gentlemen living in that district, including Melbourne, Lansdowne, and Brougham.[29] Leslie also published in the same year *A Letter to the Industrious Classes, on the Operation of the Poor Laws as Affecting Their Independence and Comfort*, a twelve-page pamphlet sold at twopence or fifteen shillings per hundred. It sketched the history and effects of the old law and explained the virtues of the new act. He summed up by saying 'The Poor Law Amendment Act was passed to restore the principles of Queen Elizabeth's Act, and to destroy the proceedings of 1795—and for what purpose? TO BENEFIT YOU,—TO IMPROVE THE CONDITION OF THE INDUSTRIOUS CLASSES OF ENGLAND.' This pamphlet was violently attacked by *Cleave's Police Gazette* for 30 January, 1835.

> Now, this friend of the industrious poor, vestryman, overseer, governor, and director, is a bold man. He takes the bull by the horns. He defends the Poor Law Robbery Bill, called an Amendment Act, upon the grounds of its utility to the plundered poor themselves. He tells them to their faces, that it is for their especial interest, for their 'independence and comfort' (no less) to be starved and imprisoned in workhouses in their old age and impotence, or to be left to starve in the streets and highways without pity and without relief from the abundance of the land, if they can get no work whilst they are able to perform it. This is the whole scope of the twelve pages of twopenny trash. . . .

Cobbett's *Poor Man's Friend* was recommended as an antidote, but, even without it, Leslie's fallacies were 'too repugnant to all good feeling and common sense to mislead any one.'[30]

So much, then, for local activity; there was publicity at the centre also. The Commission, while in many ways a 'new model' for administrative organs, had not yet acquired the modern public relations officer. They did, however, have a 'publisher by authority,' in the person of Charles Knight. He was well equipped for mass production of printed matter, and it was primarily as an administrative printer that he operated. Local production of the many forms and account books needed would have made stationery expenses of poor law authorities very great; so—charges of favouritism notwithstanding—he probably easily gained the attention of the Commission when he laid before them his plans for producing the required forms on the 'principle of cheapness.' His poor law catalogue lists general orders; instructional letters; reports of the Commission; poor law case books; guides for highway surveyors, overseers, constables, and churchwardens; poor law almanacs; information for emigrants; the *Colonization Circular* and other publications of the Colonial Land and Emigration Commission; and various forms, receipt books, and the like.[31]

The situation as regards his propagandist publishing is not so clear; information at present available makes it impossible to elucidate the precise relations between the Commission and their publisher, although it seems probable that the responsibility was almost entirely Knight's, and that initiative rarely came from the Commission. Some of the local pamphlets already cited were republished by Knight. He was responsible for the republication or sale of Head's article from the *Quarterly* and Chadwick's article from the *Edinburgh* on the progress of the law; and he saw to it that the *Companion to the Almanac* of 1837, 1838, and 1839—precisely the period of the heaviest attack on the law—was provided with long articles on the progress of the act based on reports of select committees appointed to examine the operation of the new policy. He handled the London distribution of a Manchester printed ninety-two-page pamphlet of 1837 called *A Voice from the North of England on the New Poor Laws* and directed to combatting the idea that the law was not suitable for differing conditions in the manufacturing districts. *Benevola, a Tale* came from his shop in 1840; in two parts, about a hundred pages in all and sold at three shillings and sixpence, it describes the intervention of a good fairy after whom the tale is named in affairs of the poor in England and Ireland. Needless to say, the good fairy repented her rash influence in establishing the poor laws, and was the agency for bringing the new policy into effect. The idea that Lord Brougham was subject to such influence may explain much in that strange career.

One final publication deserves some careful attention. In

1841 Knight published a 108-page duodecimo pamphlet called *Letters to Working People on the New Poor Law*. The title page proclaims that it was 'by a working man,' and it is signed John Lash Latey. Latey was a journalist who contributed to *Lloyd's News,* and who later became editor of the *Illustrated London News.*[32] In the dedication to the working men of England, Latey claims to address them 'with a respect far more profound than a titled grandee was ever addressed by the most servile worshipper of rank and riches.' He apologizes for the haste of composition which prevented polishing the text, appeals for a truth-seeking spirit, and tries to dispel the ignorance about what the law was and is.

A great deal of lackadaisical sympathy has been exhibited by the poor-law agitators, for the pauper class; whilst you, my hard-working, honest friends, who live by the sweat of your brow, who toil from morning to night, exposed to the heats of summer and the winter frosts; you, who thus labour for a scanty pittance, barely sufficient to keep body and soul together, and to obtain clothing for yourselves, and wives, and little ones, and to keep a roof over your heads; you, I say, are left almost, if not altogether, out of the question, without a single tear of pity. Pauper woes and pauper wrongs have drained their fountains dry. This whimpering over the workhouse tenant, who is better fed, better clothed, and better housed by far than the independent labourer, is to me truly sickening.

It is on this ground that he proceeds to elaborate his argument. The treatment of the lower orders in earlier periods is examined. The third letter takes up the law of settlement to illustrate the check on mobility and industry of agricultural labour, 'for labour, like water, if left to its own free course, will find its level.' Outdoor relief is the subject of letters four and five; here again the sentimentalists are berated for lamenting the passing of the well-kept pauper, when they have no tears for the downfall of the independent labourer. 'Less eligibility' is defended as a necessary safeguard against imposition by the idle. The final letter takes up the bastardy provisions and the central board, the latter receiving a remarkable amount of space, citing the obvious advantages, and rebutting charges of tyranny, unconstitutionality, and expense. His style is lively, though he has a tendency to protest over-much, to be fulsome. But the whole production misses the point. Pauperism is assumed to be a moral lapse, a lapse from peculiarly middle class virtues.

Again and again the publicists returned to the theme of the benefits of the new law, and with it was always coupled an appeal to the respectable, independent workman. It is quite true that the industrious labourer was penalized by the old system, but nothing could be more futile or more revealing of the limitations of middle class imagination than an appeal against group loyalties. Particularly was such an appeal inept when labourers in the manufacturing districts could see so clearly the limitations of an act drawn chiefly on the basis of agricultural situations and experience. In the North, where cyclical unemployment was the bugbear, the factory worker, however industrious, might be faced at any moment with a situation where he could not support himself. The fault was not his, and to talk of saving, even to the industrious, was to give counsel of perfection. He felt that he must have some rights, some right at least not to be treated as a mere counter in a bureaucratic game he did not understand.

The publications dealt with in this chapter were based largely on the practical recommendations and investigations of the commission of enquiry and of the administrative board in Somerset House; the appeal was to facts and to snobbery, and not so much to theory. It must be remembered, however, that theory—particularly the necessity of the limitation of the number of births as a pre-requisite to the favourable operation of the iron law of wages—was also a concern of the middle classes, preached by many writers. None of the little books could reconcile the working classes to the poor law as amended. It had to be changed, broadened, and humanized. It never disappeared, as most theorists thought it would do; or at any rate it did not disappear until it was effectively supplanted by a welfare state which would have been an even greater offence to most of the publicists of a hundred years ago. If the agitation died down after the forties, it was not because the working classes had been converted to the principles of 1834. The Poor Law Board could thank prosperity and the railways.

CHAPTER VII

THE THREAT OF TRADE UNIONS

THE comparative failure of the Combination Acts of 1799 and 1800, a period of prosperity and quiet, the spread of the belief in a free labour market, and some very astute political management led to the repeal of the acts in 1824; and, although the wave of strikes which followed at once led to another more restrictive act in the next year, labour moved into the crucial period of the thirties and forties with a right to combine for certain very limited purposes. There was, to be sure, a formidable array of legislation under which workmen could be prosecuted, at least indirectly, for combination or incidents arising out of combination: the master and servant laws, common-law conspiracy, and acts against illegal oaths and corresponding societies were among the major weapons of the employers and government.[1] Such dangers notwithstanding, the next two decades witnessed an amazing amount of experimentation in combination. The failures of the experiments were part of the education which is a major aspect of trade unionism and provided the materials, volcanic and sedimentary, which a sort of ice age in the fifties and sixties made into the solid unionism of the skilled trades of today.

It is intended here briefly to examine some of the appeals to the working class reader made during periods when trade union activity had impressed itself particularly on the consciousness of the middle classes. Of these periods, that of the early thirties is the most important. All the skilled trades and all areas of the country were active. The miners in the North posed a formidable threat in 1830 and 1831. The spinners of Lancashire, led by the remarkable John Doherty, staged a great strike in 1829 and moved on to a wider organization in the National Association for the Protection of Labour. Connexions were formed with midland areas and with Glasgow, where trade unionism had reached a notably mature level.

A parallel movement was developing in Yorkshire, centering about Leeds. The builders summoned their own parliament and made plans for a great guildhall in Birmingham. Some stirrings were felt even among the agricultural workers; but the conviction of the seven Tolpuddle labourers in 1834 prevented more of that sort of thing in any significant degree until the seventies. In 1833 the whole development culminated suddenly in the Grand National Consolidated Trades Union, the great all-inclusive project which incarnated the Owenism that had become the prevailing doctrine of working men, and which made Owen himself the unsuited and uncomprehending head of the movement.[2]

A token of the advance made in the organization of labour is the new articulateness of the movements of the period. The early thirties saw a wide development in short-lived but well-written and effective papers dedicated to the cause in one aspect or another. The trades council at Glasgow published the *Herald to the Trades Advocate* in 1830-31. The Owenite *Crisis*, edited by 'Shepherd' Smith, publicized the G.N.C.T.U., and Doherty was responsible for several publications, including the *Voice of the People* and the *Poor Man's Advocate*. The general radical press supported the movement and provides an important source of information today. It was in relation to James Morrison's excellent *Pioneer* of 1833-34, the organ of the builders and of the G.N.C.T.U., that the *Liverpool Standard* remarked: 'This business has reached its climax, when the Trades' Union of Birmingham has got a penny magazine of its own.'[3] Though these papers ran for only short periods, their circulation was remarkably wide; they were without any question effective agencies in spreading the doctrines of Owen and belief, according to their lights, in combination or political reform, as panaceas for working class ills.

The alarm of the government and the middle classes is reflected in the journals and in Parliament. Colonel Torrens had been working for some time on an extensive book on the financial and commercial resources of the country; but he found certain chapters on wages and combinations so applicable to the crisis that they were published separately in 1834, without waiting for the rest of the work.[4] The most celebrated and probably the most violent of the alarmist publications aimed at waking the middle classes to a clear view of the peril in which they stood, is the *Character, Object, and Effects of Trades' Unions*, published anonymously in March, 1834, by E. C. Tufnell, factory and poor law inspector. He really sums up his case in his definition of a union; it is 'a Society whose constitution is the worst of democracies—whose power is based on outrage —whose practice is tyranny—and whose end is self-destruction.'

Tufnell indicated that if the minds of workmen could be impressed with the loss of wages and with the fact that combinations had not raised, but had sometimes lowered, wages, combinations would cease to exist. How was it, asked a writer in the *Athenaeum*, that such demonstrably pernicious organizations continued to be supported? Simply because such a demonstration had not been made to the people; and he suggested a simple history of strikes written especially for the labouring classes as the most effectual means of suppressing combinations. Francis Jeffrey insisted that the true cure and preventive for the errors which led to abuses of the newly-granted freedom was to be found in a knowledge of the inexorable working of the wages fund. So too the Sheriff-substitute of Stirlingshire hoped that he would have no more cases of intimidation before him,

> and that the workmen of this country will perceive that their own and their masters' interests are one, and that every restriction they impose on the freedom of our manufactures is a blow to their prosperity, of which other countries will not be slow to avail themselves.

James Simpson referred to the danger that capital would be driven from the country by attempts to force a larger share for the workmen than they would get without force, and thought that education alone could make it clear to them how vain it is to expect to succeed in a strike in a market where numbers exceed demand. He commended Harriet Martineau's *Manchester Strike* as a demonstration of the certainty of the defeat of such aims.[5]

The S.D.U.K. was in the field in 1831 with *A Short Address to Workmen, on Combinations to Raise Wages*, obviously an attempt to parallel the success of the earlier address to agricultural labour which has already been considered. It was written by Henry Gawler, at the request of that most active and righteous member of the Society, Henry Bellenden Ker,[6] published as a twelve-page pamphlet at a penny, with, as usual, a reduction for purchase in quantities. The Society authorized the reprinting of the pamphlet by anyone 'who may think it useful.' To judge from the relative silence of the Society's letters, the pamphlet did not meet with the hoped-for success, although the packets sent to correspondents were undoubtedly distributed in the hope of accomplishing some good.[7] The magistrates at Wrexham in North Wales requested the local committee of the S.D.U.K. to have the *Address* translated into Welsh for distribution among the colliers and miners who were unable to read English, and hoped to arrange a general Welsh distribution to combat the extensive combination in existence in the principality. The local distribution was expected to be financed out of sales to the magistrates and masters; and if the Committee found it impossible to further the extension of the work, it was to be disposed of to a bookseller.[8]

The address is interesting as an example of the purely theoretical approach; there is no attempt made to illustrate the propositions advanced by reference to the history of combinations. While the avowed objects of unions seem innocent enough, if success cannot be obtained without violating the principles of freedom, justice, and the rights of others, then, Gawler maintains, they are only steps to tyranny. Infringements of the prevailing principles of entire security for personal freedom and unfettered use of property, labour, and industry can never be of advantage. The principles of combinations lead to the destruction of property, the decline of profit, and the transfer of capital to more secure countries. The existence of occasional distress is admitted, but he will not allow that distress is due to the selfishness of employers; rather it is the outcome of fluctuations of markets, and wages depend on these, not on the will of employers. 'When the labour offered for sale is plentiful its price will be low, when it is scarce it will be high. . . . This is the law of nature, against which it is in vain to contend.' And the evils which workmen suffer might well be lessened in part by 'forbearance, management, and economy.' Frequently the author stoops to the sneering manner encountered before, which would certainly have done as much as the assumptions to infuriate a working class reader, if such were to be found. No man likes to be told that his complaints are exaggerated or that he is a dupe 'of the few well-paid artisans who can always find work.' At the request of the Committee of the Society in April, 1834, Gawler revised the address, but the sudden collapse of the Grand National and the whole combination movement removed the urgency, and the Publication Committee decided in July that another address at that time would be inexpedient.[9]

In March, 1833, W. B. Baring, on the advice of Birkbeck and Nassau Senior, sent on to the Society an essay on combinations by one Charles Fines, which had won a prize at the London Mechanics' Institution in the previous month. Baring thought that it should be headed so as to indicate its source, for 'such a work so headed would circulate among the working classes of England with greater authority, and more extensively than anything proceeding from the pen of an abstract reasoner.' A different method might perhaps be more suitable for men of education, but 'the analytical mode of procedure is by far easier and more attractive to those unaccustomed to abstract studies.' Furthermore, such a publication would encourage intellectual pursuits among the labouring population as well as communicate knowledge. But apparently the Committee disagreed with the three sponsors, and nothing came of their suggestion.[10] The *Penny Magazine* during these years showed no trace of the combination problem, but *Chambers's Edinburgh Journal* did not feel the scruples of its competitors; at any rate an article on the evils of combination, with a long quotation from Babbage, appeared in the issue of 28 September, 1833, while on 7 December an extract was published from *Hints to the Working Classes, Explanatory of Their True Interests, and the Effects of Trade Unions.*

Knight himself, his connexion with the S.D.U.K. aside, was not content to let matters rest. In his *Companion to the Newspaper* for July, 1833, he announced that, in view of the general resort to combination, some steps had to be taken to inform workmen as to their own real interests, and that his paper would contribute to this work whenever the occasion arose. Owen had broached his idea of a Grand National Moral Union in October, 1833; the Society for National Regeneration was founded in Lancashire in November; and strikes had been frequent throughout the year. More significant was the fact that by the end of the year, starting in Leicestershire and Derbyshire, the employers had begun to counter-attack, and lock-outs spread over the whole country. Clearly the occasion offered, and in the December issue of the *Companion* there was a long article on trade unions, following the usual line—the right to combine is undoubted, but some of the actions of unions are to be deplored. The emphasis is on the necessity of limiting the number of labourers, by going out of the market; the price of unskilled labour can be raised only by the increase of capital and the diffusion of knowledge; but when machinery is used to the utmost, there will be no more unskilled labour, and the evils of that part of society will vanish.

This article roused the wrath of Francis Place; his condemnation, in a letter to Parkes, must be quoted at length:

The matter you suggested to me has, I see, been accomplished; Trades Unions are treated of in the *Companion to the Newspaper*, for the 1st December, done too exactly in the way I expected. In a very absurd way certainly, and in a bad spirit. If it is intended for the working people, nothing can be more foolish. Not a working man will read it without condemning it, and looking upon the writer as his enemy; he will see that it is a one-sided paper, that he is treated as an irrational creature, and he will be more than ever confirmed in his false notions. The folly of the writer and his supporters is surprising. *He* understands the subject and, much as I conclude he desires to be extensively read by the working classes, he takes especial care to defeat his own purpose. There is much good and some excellent matter in his essay, but it is sadly prosy, just the reverse of what a paper should be as to style, to intice [sic] men on and compel them to come to right conclusions. There is a wandering, a beating about the bush which is sure to create suspicion, that all is not right, that something wrong is intended which cannot fail to create a prejudice against the writer; thus the reader, if a working man, will be made to suspect something amiss before he comes to the most interesting part of the subject, and when he gets there he will find an absurd and broad distinction which he will at once condemn as a false shewing. He will find that all the masters [are] wise men, all the work people [are] fools. He will find all the actions of the masters represented as just; all those of the workmen as unjust. This surely never could have been the intention of the writer, if he meant to address himself to the working people.

He then proceeded to examine the discussion of various strikes in which the men were invariably shown at fault, whereas in reality in every case the men were locked out.

Every such essay as this, makes it more and more difficult to drum sound doctrine into the people, and helps to a prodigious extent such strange creatures as John Fielden, Esq., M.P., and Old ignorance Cobbett, M.P., to lead the people astray. They on one side and our essay writer on the other side, are enough to keep up the deplorable contention, and would if it were possible produce civil war in the land. I do think that if it were possible, which happily it is not, that a commotion could take place, it would be no more than strict justice to hang these three men.[11]

This restatement of Knight's formula of going out of the market, already seen in the *Results of Machinery*, was not the full extent of his contribution to the crisis. The Tufnell pamphlet appeared in March of 1834, and was reviewed in the *Times* on 3 April; in May appeared an anonymous volume called *Trades Unions and Strikes*, which Knight hurriedly produced, partly by extracting the Tufnell pamphlet *verbatim*, and partly by dependence on other writers.[12] This little publication —ninety-nine pages for sixpence—is a bit chaotic and repetitive and gives the impression of very rapid compilation. But its aim is clear—to show the invariable failure of strikes. If workmen could be brought to realize that wages are reduced only under necessity, the poverty and misery arising from strikes would be avoided. Further, strikes accelerate the introduction of machinery, so that the worker loses any possibility of returning to work. The final section is devoted to the law of combinations, and the conclusion drawn is that entry into any *large* combination is a dangerous course, that scarcely any amount of circumspection can save the members from criminal responsibility in one form or another.

Place's pamphleteering in connexion with the combination movement is most instructive. In November of 1833 he was approached by Joseph Parkes with the suggestion that he write a penny paper to be published periodically at no expense to the author, presumably by the government, for whose members Parkes frequently acted as agent. Place replied that he would gladly do so, if he could be certain that he would not lose his time. He intended to do justice to both sides, and he doubted that Parkes's clients would print such a composition. Here the matter rested until December, when Place re-opened negotiations as a result of the infuriating article in the *Companion to the Newspaper*. The upshot of all this negotiation was four pamphlets. Parkes, while declaring himself pleased with them, did not feel able to show them to his clients and turned instead to the S.D.U.K. Here he was defeated by Bellenden Ker, who was afraid of identifying the Society with Place's embarrassing views on birth control, and by the secretary, Thomas Coates, who objected to Place's publication of the correspondence with the Society, cited in an earlier chapter, concerning a mechanics' reading room. Parkes then turned to Knight, who agreed to print the essays on Parkes's description. Place, however, knew that, once Knight actually saw the pamphlets, he would have nothing to do with them. Furthermore, Knight was not a suitable publisher;

> . . . they must be published by Hetherington, Steill, and Watson. They are intended for the deluded workmen, not for their masters and their calumniators. The Unionists will read nothing which the Diffusion Society meddles with. They call the members of it Whigs, and the word whig with them, means a treacherous rascal, a bitter, implacable enemy. It is their own fault much more than it is the fault of the working people that this mischievous animosity exists. Companion to Newspapers—Report of Factory Commissioners, Tuffnell's [sic] pamphlet, etc., etc., and

ministers more deluded and more silly, than the uninformed mass, making Dorchester displays have done the mischief. . . .

Parkes returned the manuscripts, and plans which some of Place's friends suggested for raising money to publish them apparently came to nothing.[13]

In the pamphlets Place deals hardly in all directions. The upper classes are denounced for their partial views, the injustice of their generalizing, and their inability or refusal to see the peculiarities of the position of the workmen, condemning in them the same procedures considered laudable in their own 'trades unions.' The last tract, indeed, is a discussion of these upper class 'unions'—the Board of Agriculture, the bar, and the municipal corporations. The working classes, on the other hand, are told that their Owenite objects and their demands at the present juncture for an eight-hour day are chimerical. Trades clubs—open, continuous, respectable, and limited to purely economic and educational purposes—are as strongly defended as the combination laws are denounced. If it were not for the existence of trades clubs, all labour would be in the position of the unorganized agricultural labourers and at the mercy of masters from whom nothing can be expected. But trades unions—composed of portions of several trades working through delegates, subject to momentary enthusiasms, possessed of a kind of German *mystique*—are unreservedly condemned; they are really political unions under another name, and for unattainable objects. Trades clubs cannot, of course, annul the laws of political economy. Again and again Place insisted that political economists are the friends, not the enemies, of workmen, and that the wages fund theory must be their basic reliance.

It is understandable why these pamphlets were never published. Place was quite right in supposing that Parkes's 'masters' would have nothing to do with them, for he upheld combination as necessary, criticized the ill-informed opposition to it, and denounced the writer in the *Companion to the Newspaper*, Tufnell, and the factory commissioners for their partiality and confusion. But he was also running counter to working class feeling at the time. That he recognized this is shown in the second tract, where he mentions that he will not please and begs for a hearing on the basis of his years of service to working class interests. The lessons of 1834 were the virtue of combination and the realization *through experience* of the impossibility of the utopian schemes—results which could hardly have been affected one way or the other by Knight or Tufnell or even Place. But Place wrote as a man possessed of truth and convinced of the power of reason, once the breach in prejudice was made.

With combinations, as with any subject touching on political economy, one must reckon with Harriet Martineau; and, as always, her efforts are highly instructive, because they are pretty thoroughly documented. It will be remembered that she had written *The Rioters*, a tale on machine-breaking and industrial disturbance, for a Wellington publisher in 1827; this was so successful that she was requested by a group of Derby and Nottingham manufacturers to do a similar tale on the subject of wages. The result of this collaboration with employers and manufacturers—not her last—was *The Turn-Out; or, Patience the Best Policy*. Printed in 1829, it contains one hundred and thirty-five pages, and sold for a shilling and sixpence. Like her later and better *Manchester Strike* in the political economy series, this tale centres about a strike leader who is made to witness the hardships caused by the turn-out, and whose support falls away. The climax is a great meeting in which Henry's oratory is overcome by the good sense spoken by the enlightened manufacturer, Mr. Wallace, on the importance of capital and of obedience to economic laws.

After the tremendous success of the series of political economy tales, Harriet Martineau found herself not only a constant diner-out in the best society, but an authority on the fashionable science and ways of disseminating it. Among the friendships formed at this period was one with Lord Durham, the most promising figure in the radical wing of the Whig party, and the owner of extensive coal properties on the Tyne, managed by his agent, Morton. Labour difficulties were chronic in the northern coal fields during the early thirties; and Durham invited the young authoress to make her contribution to their solution, supplying her with 'a good deal of information respecting the system of strikes, unions, delegates, and the like amongst the miners, which I am sure she can work up well.' The outcome was the little pamphlet, *The Tendency of Strikes and Sticks to Produce Low Wages, and of Union between Masters and Men to Ensure Good Wages*, published at Durham in 1834. Durham wrote to Harriet that he would

> see Mr. Morton, and arrange with him as to the best mode of circulating it. Its style and tone is [sic] perfectly adapted to win the confidence and convince the understandings of the working classes. No time is to be lost, for on the Tyne the combination is spreading rapidly, and the most violent and bloody measures are openly avowed.[14]

The pamphlet starts out by picturing the evils of trade fluctuations, which mean eventually the necessity of discharging some men or of lowering the wages of all, the latter certainly being preferable. Now, in such an instance, where the workman's case is undeniably hard, it is his right and duty to investigate the case and to seek a remedy. To this end he will consult with his fellows, for, if anything is to be done, acting in concert will make it more effectual. If oppressed, they can best resist oppression by being combined; and, if the masters are not to blame, they can help each other and refrain from underbidding. In the situation of 1834, the state of trade is open knowledge. Competition is severe, and the margin of profit is dangerously narrow or even in some cases non-existent. An opposition of interests at such a time will only mean the loss of subsistence to all parties; a common front of masters and men will enable both to ride the storm. Strikes may succeed for a while, but, unless trade improves greatly, the consequences are bound to be bad in the end. She then turns to examples, showing the substitution of other labourers and of machinery. The tremendous waste in supporting the idle is pointed out, as are the heavy delegate expenses and the misuse of funds by unwise or untrustworthy leaders. In the end, the argument comes down to freedom of bargaining and the surplus of labour; the recommendation, the store of savings which Knight recommended, and which Durham hoped to implement with a pension and insurance scheme. Workers should combine against ill fortune, not against their masters.

Place, who approved of Lord Durham's benefit scheme,

called the pamphlet 'good, very good,' and promised to do all he could to help its circulation, by distributing a large number both among leaders of workmen and in his own name.[15] But Place was in a minority. The tract may or may not have helped the situation in County Durham; certainly it did little to help the author's reputation. The *Athenaeum*, having urged a simple history of strikes, sadly concluded that this work did not fulfil the purpose; either the author had been spoiled by praise or was over-writing herself, 'for the work is mere dogmatizing on pompous nothings, instead of reasoning, as was her custom, on simple truths.'[16] Perhaps more wounding to her was the review in her own *Monthly Repository*, from the hand of her mentor, W. J. Fox, a review which saw through the defects of Harriet's enthusiasm to the hard core of the problem of popular writing. 'She claims to be a teacher of the people; and well has her claim been supported by most of her works. But to be the people's teacher she must always show herself the people's friend, not merely for the soundness of her advice, but by the tone and spirit of her admonitions.'[17]

A tale worth noting is part three, *The Trades' Unionist*, of a series by the Glasgow bookseller, John Reid, called *Illustrations of Social Depravity*, and appropriately published in 1834. The chief character is an enlightened gentleman who converts two unionists in a small town, and later defends the principles of combination for properly limited purposes to an irascible anti-union employer. The latter thinks that government should cure the disturbances by the sword, but Johnson urges that the true way to put down unions is for employers to unite to grant just and refuse unjust demands. Then the power of the unions ' would melt away like snow beneath a tropical sun.' Finally, the crisis of 1834, like other crises, turned up its dialogue. *The Strike: or, a Dialogue between Andrew Plowman and John Treadle*, was published by Thomas Hookham in London in 1834, and in it, as usual, the worthy and unsophisticated countryman puts down the superficial, enthusiastic mechanic. When John reminds Andrew that he has said that it is in the master's interest to keep wages down, and asks how he can be sure that his master is not giving lower wages than he can afford, Andrew admits an inability to answer without a greater knowledge than he has—a convenient, if hardly satisfactory, manner for an author to pass over a point.

> But my argument [says Andrew] is this: You have no right to insist upon your master paying you higher wages, if he can find a man who can supply your place for lower wages; nor have you a right to say to that man, that he shall not work for such wages as he likes himself, but at such wages as you like. And I repeat my former observation, that to insist on your master advancing your wages, without knowing whether he can afford it or not, is the very height of injustice. I have never attended any *economy* lectures, John, as you have done, and maybe know little of the matter; but, in my humble opinion, there should be no combinations, either of masters or of servants. The master should be free to hire servants (pardon me, John, I should have said *operatives*) at the lowest wages he can, without any secret understanding between him and other masters, and the operatives—the operatives, John, should be at liberty, each to engage for himself to work for such wages, as he is willing to take.
>
> J. Well, Andrew, I am not sure but that would be the fairest and best plan after all. . . .[18]

1837 and 1838 saw trade unions again strongly impressed on the awareness of the middle classes, partly by the trial of the Glasgow cotton spinners, partly by the select committee which O'Connell demanded and got in the latter year. G. R. Porter, at work on his *Progress of the Nation* and having a good vantage point in his position at the Board of Trade, was worried by the symptoms of discontent. He brought the matter to the council of the new Statistical Society of London, of which he was a leading member, and a committee was appointed. Porter made clear to Place what he wanted:

> We shall go to work promptly and vigorously for the collection of facts, with the hope that when these are brought to the knowledge of the employers and the workmen, the worse than useless nature of [combination] will be apparent, that the masters on one hand may be led to make such

timely concessions as can fairly be expected, while the men may be induced to pause before they enter upon combinations that must be fraught with so much evil to them.

The principal reliance of the committee was a questionnaire sent to reliable persons in the industrial areas. The fifty-seven questions covered such matters as organization of labour, the causes and duration of recent strikes, the condition of the working people, and the terms of employment before and after the strike. When those questions were answered, Porter told Place, 'it will be quite open to us . . . then to go into other branches of the enquiry, and for one I shall be very desirous to do so.' Apparently considerable information was collected, but, like so many projects of the Statistical Society, it has left no trace. The statistical proof of the futility of combination was never issued to the public, but Porter's concern over the problem is revealing enough to be noted here.[19]

In January, 1838, the Edinburgh Association of the Working Classes, for their Intellectual, Moral, and Social Improvement heard a lecture by James Taylor on *The Effects of Combinations and Strikes on the Welfare of the Working Classes*, the substance of which was subsequently published at the request of the Association by A. and C. Black. The first part of the pamphlet is given over to a discussion of the wages fund theory, and the futility of combinations to keep up the price of labour in view of the consequent reduction of capital and hampering of the competitive position of the country. He also attacks the limitation of apprenticeship and the fixing of a minimum wage. But he sees that the unjust and unreasoned prejudice against political economy will prevent the due effect of arguments based on it, so the rest of the pamphlet is taken up with illustrations of the failure of unions; he bases his case on Babbage, Ure, Harriet Martineau, and Wade's *History*. *Chambers's Journal* cited the little pamphlet as a useful compilation of instances of the folly of combination, and quoted at length from it in one of their articles on the subject.[20]

Another local production of 1838 which deserves mention is *An Affectionate Warning to the Agricultural Labourers in the Parish of Preston-cum-Sutton, in the County of Dorset*, sold in Weymouth and Dorchester. It is the substance of a sermon against the endeavours of certain persons who had come into the parish to urge combination to raise wages and lower the price of bread. The incumbent, the Rev. Octavius Piers, does not argue political economy to his parishioners; he assigns two reasons why they should not permit themselves to be led astray. The means proposed are ungodly, unscriptural, and, if generally adopted, productive of 'the most awful consequences throughout the kingdom; and the objects are utterly impracticable. '. . . Such a state of things as *cheap bread* and *high wages* for the Agricultural Labourers *never had*, and *never could* exist in this world. . . .' His support is not Harriet Martineau, but the Bible. It is a small, almost parenthetical, publication; but it is interesting as it shows the continued use of the old-fashioned appeal, and the persistence of a drive to combination in rural society, four years after the transportation of the Dorchester labourers had presumably demonstrated that one segment of society must remain uninfected.

The forties produced a fairly steady crop of anti-union literature. There was a pamphlet called *Wages*, addressed to 'the honest and industrious Operatives of Manchester, especially those engaged in the Cotton Trade,' published by Gadsby the anti-corn-law publisher, in 1842. Still another publication from the same background of unrest was *A Bit o' Talk between a Turnout and One Who Has Gone Back to His Work*. Houlston, in Wellington, reprinted Harriet Martineau's 1827 tale, *The Rioters*, with unauthorized changes to adapt it to the times. In Edinburgh in 1843-4, James Simpson gave a series of lectures to the working classes, one of which was devoted to the laws of wages and the futility of attempting to raise them above their natural level by combination.[21]

A considerable amount of material relating to a specific industrial crisis in the forties is preserved and is probably typical of similar upheavals as stimuli to appeals to the working classes. In April of 1844 the miners of Durham and Northumberland came out on strike, their ultimate resort in a long dispute with coal-owners over the terms of the bond, fines, and wages. It was the second union, the first having failed in the early thirties after a brief success. The second was even less successful than the first. The general nature of the strike prevented contributions on working miners for the benefit of strikers.

Union funds had been used to a considerable extent in financing legal proceedings conducted by W. P. Roberts, the Bath attorney and Chartist turned 'miners' attorney-general.' The owners, better prepared, were assiduous in bringing in strangers to the pits; and by the end of July such men as could be rehired had returned to their work. The strike was useful, however, in placing the miners' case before the public, who were impressed by the generally high level of conduct displayed. And the loyalty the men showed to the cause until crushed by hunger and eviction was a stimulus to further attempts at union.[22]

Certainly the miners were more articulate in this strike than in the previous one. The press was generally against them,[23] but, in addition to the major publicizing device of the great public meeting, the miners had a very vigorous and well-run unstamped paper, edited by William Daniells, called the *Miners' Advocate*. The first issue, 2 December, 1843, consisted of eight pages and sold for three halfpence. It appeared fortnightly until 27 July, 1844, when a prosecution was brought for infringement of the stamp laws, whereupon it began to appear monthly. A new series began in May, 1845, which ran to April, 1846, when an interruption took place. This time the paper retreated, like many other radical papers, to Douglas in the Isle of Man, where it could have the twin advantage of freedom from the stamp laws and free distribution through the Post Office. The paper was first-rate agitation, with heavy emphasis on mine safety. During the strike it devoted itself to answering the attacks made on the miners by the regular newspapers, particularly the *Newcastle Advertiser* and the *Durham Chronicle*. Tremenheere had something to say about it and its predecessor, the *Miners' Journal*:

They were both conducted by working men, well known in that part of the country, and many of the contributions were evidently the compositions of men of that grade of life. Among these were not wanting some which manifested excellent feeling, and aspirations which under better opportunities of sound instruction would have been conducted into right channels. But the mass of both publications consisted of assertions hazarded without examination, imputations of dishonourable and unchristian motives freely cast upon those above them, distortions of facts, and general reasonings calculated to mislead the ignorant. Some months of excitement, kept up by these publications, and by frequent public meetings, produced their effect. The main topics in both were—first, the policy of a general and simultaneous cessation from labour throughout the whole of the coal-districts of the kingdom; and secondly, the various alleged local grievances, relative to wages, fines, the mode of weigh-ing, the ventilation of the pits, etc. . . . No arguments had any chance of obtaining access to their minds, except those suggested to them by their own periodical, and by the delegates who addressed them. The fallacies by which they were misled, few among them were capable of seeing through.[24]

The paper was not the sole publication of the miners. Daniells also compiled a *Miners' Almanack* for 1844, along lines similar to other almanacs used for propaganda purposes. It contained twenty-four pages and sold at a penny; besides the usual almanac information and references to events and dates important to radicals, there was a grim list of explosions and accidents in mines in the Durham and Northumberland field from 1658 to 1844, and a scheme for ventilating mines. Two other pamphlets were *An Essay on the Abridgment of the Hours of Labour in Mines, Pits, etc.*, a prize essay by Robert Forbes, a miner of Newarthill, published at Coatbridge; and *The Question Answered: 'What Do the Pitmen Want?'* by William Mitchell, a pitman of Ouston Colliery, published in at least three editions at Bishopwearmouth. The volume in the Newcastle Public Library which contains these and all the items mentioned here also contains several handbills put out by the Miners' Associa-tion on attempts of coalowners to recruit labour, for example, 'A Dialogue between Three Coal Viewers after Being in Search of Men.' There are also several ballad slips, among which are 'A Song to the Blacklegs and All Those Not in the Union,' and 'Mr. Roberts, the Pitmen's Friend.'[25]

The other side turned to newspapers, pamphlets, and hand-bills to state their case to the striking miners. A favourite line of attack, as in all industrial disputes, was to suggest that the leaders of the union were self-interested men who had fastened on the miners as a means of support. The Newcastle volume contains an unidentified newspaper cutting of a letter to the pitmen of the West Hartlepool district, dated 22 May and signed 'A Colliery Agent'; it is an attack on Roberts, accusing him of taking vast sums for no return. Roberts was also the object of a demand for an accounting in a handbill headed 'To the Pitmen of Thornley Colliery,' and signed 'One who is tiring of the Union.' A handbill published in March was headed 'A Few Friendly Words to the Pitmen of Durham and North-umberland,' and signed 'A Friend to both Coalowner and Pitman.' This writer too attacks the leaders, though he disclaims imputing insincerity to them:

> . . . you are paying these men for embroiling you with your employers, and for the poor privilege of being made discontented and unhappy by their continual croaking about evils which are, after all, only the penalty of Adam, shared by you in common with the vast majority of mankind.

His points are three: first, that they are better paid than any other class of colliers in Great Britain and that they must beware the masters watching them 'with the steady eye of power,' who might take the opportunity to overwhelm them; second, that coal-mining is no mystery, and that people come into the industry not only as blacklegs in time of strike, but also simply by transfer from other occupations; and third, that the irregularity of their work is due to excessive numbers.

> I pray of you to take my observations, as they are intended in good faith. Admitting your undoubted right to sell your labour to the best advantage, my wish is to shew that its value depends upon circumstances, over which neither you nor your employers have a control, and to convince you that it is not by acting in opposition to them you can ever gain any thing, but by uniting with them, as persons should do who are in the same boat together, and identified by a strong common interest.

The appeal to political economy, implicit here, is clearer in a huge broadside headed 'On Trades Unions and Strikes,' which was not concerned directly with the strike, but with a

larger attack on combination as tyrannical, unfair to the superior
workman, and injurious to trade.

A small handbill, dated 18 May and headed 'May a Christian
Join the Union,' returns an unequivocal no to its question, as
any ostensible good the union might do could be accomplished
only by overwhelming evil to property owners, families, other
workmen, creditors, society, and to the worker's own morals,
self-respect, and soul. John Besley, vicar of St. Andrew, Long
Benton, preached a sermon on 9 June, on *The Respective Duties
of Master and Servant*, published as a sixteen-page pamphlet at
Long Benton. Much of it is taken up with explanation of
passages in Scripture urging unity and the justice required of
the employers, but stressing, above all, the 'diligence, fidelity,
and submission' required of servants. The incumbent of
Castle Eden put out a handbill on the first of May. The Rev.
John Burdon concentrated in this essay on three points, the
influx of new hands, the foolishness of restricting earnings, and
the flouting of the will of God in the strike. In late June,
Burdon, then removed to London, addressed another handbill 'To the Pitmen of the Wingate Grange and Castle Eden
Collieries.' He admitted that his previous address had given
great offence, and he doubted whether anger against him had
entirely subsided. But he was determined to be heard, and his
message contained much more political economy than his
first effort. The necessity for security of capital and arguments
from loss of wages and suffering made up his chief talking
points. *An Address to the Rev. John Burdon* is a twelve-page
reply published in Newcastle, a rather crudely written pamphlet
answering the clergyman point by point, and ending by
denouncing

all your flummery of kindest and best intentions. . . . Oh
what exquisite feelings—truly a man of feeling—feelings
by the dozen—its all a fudge Mr. Burdon and will not fit,
there is too much subtle serpentism about it, the cloak is
too short, and the cloven foot appears from beneath its
skirt.

One last project must be referred to. It will be recalled that
Harriet Martineau worked with Lord Durham and his man-
ager, Morton, in the 1834 troubles to produce *Strikes and*

Sticks. A common interest in education also led to a friendship between her and Seymour Tremenheere. Tremenheere, in fact, turned the first spade of earth for her new house at Ambleside, but the friendship was badly strained by her association with the Howitts in the *People's Journal* in 1846 and was completely broken by her virtual conversion to free-thought. But in 1844 they were friends and colleagues. Apparently Tremenheere, or some of the employers to whom he talked, had the idea of a Newcastle periodical to be published as an antidote to the *Miners' Advocate*. Harriet Martineau, at this time bedridden in Tynemouth, received the suggestion with enthusiasm. She wanted some specific information about truck and fines and so on, and she had questions about other things. Was the paper to be for that district alone or to include the Northwest and Staffordshire? What was to be its title and form? From what quarters was it to appear to proceed? Was it to avow its antagonism to the *Advocate*?

> I see in these papers a wholesome tendency to speculate on the possible exhaustion of coal in this country. I could use this speculation to good purpose. There is a good deal about Pennsylvania Coal and mining and the rate of wages there. Do you think readers would be entertained with a short series of Letters as from a Pennsylvania Miner? Much capital instruction might, I think, be conveyed in this form, —Labour having the upper hand over Capital in America, yet being manifestly helpless by itself. My American Journal is in the closet here, and I could make the scene thoroughly Pennsylvanian. I traversed the State twice, and saw the Alleghany [sic] Miners.

Possibly 'Morton and his crowd' could answer these questions, but one other point only Tremenheere could answer. It seemed to her quite clear that the hatred the men felt for the viewers was reciprocated; therefore, while they might correct anything she wrote as to matters of fact or even verbal style, she could not agree to any hardening or sharpening of what she said.

> My sympathies *are* with the ignorant and misled; and I *am* on their side, as far as their general *human* claims go. I have not the least doubt that these gentlemen are so too,

in the abstract: but I *must* harp upon the men's own favourite terms and ideas, which I know are wearisome and nauseous to their employers; and what I say must stand. For one illustration 'Union is strength,' they say:—but every viewer quivers at the word Union. I shall adopt the saying,—enforce it, urge it home: and *then* show that Union of all the necessary parts to an achievement is the thing meant: and that 'union' to set one element against another is truly 'division.' (All in the most familiar mode, of course). Now if these gentlemen take me for a mouthpiece, they must let me supply the *morale* of the matter. About the *doctrine*, they and I are agreed; and I thankfully abandon the *facts* to them.

It was in connexion with this proposed series that Harriet Martineau had her idea for explaining the development of the British Constitution, already discussed in an earlier chapter.

Support from Morton, Colonel Grey, Lady Mary Lambton, and other prominent persons in the area was promised; but apparently other difficulties intervened. The Newcastle project was abandoned for a publication by the Chambers brothers, but the Chamberses could not promise to undertake any such project for some time because of the press of other business, and information on the final disposition of the scheme is not to be found.[26]

Education was, however, to be a primary solvent for the troubles in the coal fields. One need only turn over the pages of Tremenheere's reports for the next few years to note the great activity in setting up schools and libraries in mining areas, but his steady concern about the nature of the reading material circulating among the working classes indicates the problems facing the disseminators of old and new orthodoxies converging on the fifties. They could see that they had far to go. Perhaps the challenge in its nature implied defeat.

CONCLUSION

THE response to the challenge offered by the working class reader was two-fold. In its first stage, which lasted through the post-war crises, it was puzzlement, agitation, and opposition. Established means of communication, such as later newspapers and magazines provided, were nearly unknown. Crises were dealt with as they came; humour, scurrility, and denunciation were the chief devices, along with the equally venerable practice of preaching religion and morality to accomplish social purposes. The second stage was entered as the middle classes found new confidence in themselves and new respect for the working classes, extorted by intellectual power or sheer numbers. Old-fashioned methods continued to be used, but from the twenties the noteworthy efforts were primarily preventive, not defensive. Newspapers and magazines were more widely established and available; but, even where the weapons were the same—tracts, broadsides, tales, and so on—the materials and the techniques were often different from those of the earlier period. Perhaps the most significant change was the new emphasis on the laws of political economy, whose truth had to be demonstrated and whose rule had to be assured.

The problem of communication in all these efforts was likewise two-fold. It was first a problem in techniques. It was necessary to keep the price down, and, wherever possible in this study, prices of pamphlets have been mentioned to offer some gauge of their availability to the working classes. The problem of price has been posed, but not discussed in detail; for, the question of taxation aside, it is a matter primarily for a badly needed economic history of popular publishing which this study makes no pretence at being. Paper-making, the expansion of the printing industry, and the economics of distribution are questions apart. But one question of distribution has been present at every turn; where price was prohibitive, as it generally was, or where interest was not sufficient to lead the working classes to purchase, or where the urgency of a crisis demanded a speedy intervention, resort was had to free distribution by the middle and upper classes. To emphasize this factor, wherever the situation presented itself, the price has been given for the publication both singly and in lots for distribution. This reliance is of very great importance and has been stressed because it was inevitable and because it contributed to the failure of most of the enterprises. Charles Knight had realized that when the *Plain Englishman* failed. He wrote in 1828 that

> no scheme for the diffusion of popular knowledge can be successful which is not immediately addressed to the people themselves, without in any degree depending upon the patronage of gratuitous, and therefore suspicious distribution, by the superiors of those for whose perusal works of a popular character are devised.[1]

But his own organization, the Society for the Diffusion of Useful Knowledge, was entirely dependent on upper class support, both financially and administratively, a dependence which hampered its operation and inhibited its circulation.

Another set of persistent problems in technique were concerned with attracting the interest of the working man and with pitching the productions on the right level and in the proper style to hold and convince him. Here, from the outset, attempts were made to mimic the popular literature of the day, by putting out moral or conservative tracts in the form of chapbooks. As the chapbook disappeared, the format of the improving productions tended to change to mimic the popular journals and, when the laws did not interfere, as they usually did, the newspapers which were the mainstay of the working class reader. Broadsides were a continual device, eye-catching and concise. Tales, dialogues, and parables were used to accommodate instruction to popular taste for narrative. Here too is the beginning of illustration, both as an impetus to reading and as a means of instruction; the suggestive crude woodcuts of the pseudo-chapbooks gave way to the expert wood engraving of the *Penny Magazine*, but the important development in this field fell well after mid-century with the advent of photography, photo-engraving, and colour printing.

The problems of level and style were much more elusive to the middle class educators. Continually before them were the stunning examples of working class writers, of whom Cobbett was the greatest, whose style was perfectly adapted to get across to their tremendous followings. Many people realized perfectly well the desiderata—simplicity, lack of affectation, comprehensiveness, familiarity, manliness, avoidance of condescension, or whatever terms might be found to describe the indescribable.[2] Attaining them was all but impossible, for respectability and lack of contact stood in the way.

The second aspect of the problem of communication was one of understanding, and it was this fault that was gravest of all, this obstacle the least able to be surmounted. A writer in the *Westminster Review* urged that would-be popular writers acquaint themselves with workmen and workshops. Such an experience would be of advantage to their pupils and to themselves as well.

> And if among them are any who have not hitherto formed this acquaintance, we can assure them that they will not find it the disagreeable society which they may have expected, and which too many are apt to imagine. So far from this, they will often have occasion to discover a degree of information, as well as of intelligence, which will convince them that they have not undertaken to teach children or savages; and with that, a frequent tone of far better feeling, and also of better manners, than those persons expect who know nothing of the lower orders but that they are not so well dressed as ourselves, and drink porter in lieu of wine.[3]

Here was the really significant cause of the failure of these attempts to diffuse useful knowledge or to combat error by truth. The great part of the working classes, like the great part of any class, were not actively interested in learning; they wanted to be amused, and were so in one way or another. Such ideas as they had in political and social matters came, not from the exercise of reason, but from experience, economic necessity, a vague but important sense of justice and dignity, a preference for collective action, and infection by better-informed and more active fellow workers. For the latter, the diffusion attempts were quite useless.

It is evidently unnecessary for Societies and Reviewers, and Diffusionists, and Philosophers, and all the rest of us, to talk about enlightening the operatives, and instructing the mass of the population. We may go to sleep, so far as that is concerned. They will not wait for our instructions. They will instruct themselves; and 'tis odds but they teach us something also. The 'great moral lessons' are not all learned yet. What with their suspicions and our inaptitude, we may as well give over adult school-keeping. The 'Diffusion' political economy, so well meant, and so clumsily executed, was alone enough to cut the connexion. 'Take yourselves out of the labour market,' said the philosophers. 'Take yourselves out of the rostrum,' replied the mechanics. They are self-sufficient; and until far other instructors appear than most of those who have yet manifested themselves, we cannot blame them for being so. Prophets are raised up to them 'of their own brethren,' and why should they listen to the voice of the stranger? Their souls have found congenial interpreters. The oracles of inspiration are uttered in their own language. Let them teach one another. They will get at truth all the same; alloyed perhaps at first with error, and discoloured by bitter indignation, but still truth.[4]

The analysis is brilliant. The middle classes were doomed to defeat from the outset.

In reality, the challenge of the working class reader is best seen from another angle than that of the intended audience, who could take care of themselves and did so. As it has appeared in this book, the response has been shown increasingly as a drive to proselytizing which came with the growing confidence, the mushrooming sense of moral superiority, the sublime convictions of the British middle classes. All classes and all nations, in their ascendancies, view history as a kind of Hegelian dialectic stopping providentially and inevitably with themselves, projecting their own society infinitely into the future. History is a series of lessons in humility, learned and then forgotten. Here was perhaps the most astonishing ascendancy of a class ever seen, and here too were the moral blemishes that go with such ascendancy. It was the conviction of these middle class enthusiasts that the world, or, as a good and vital start, the English working classes were to be made over in their image. And they set to propagating all their ideas. They propagated religion, morals, art, temperance, charity, respectability, prudence, emigration, progress, and political economy; and, because snobbery is operative at every social level, because the Kenwigs were as plentiful in England as they are evident in *Nicholas Nickleby*, success was theirs in some fields. But the working classes generally were to hammer out their own society, their own culture, and not to take it by impregnation or battering from above. And the middle classes, with the best will in the world, made certain their own defeat. They were condescending and condemnatory when they had no intention of being so. They tried to impose their standards and criteria on people whose needs were different. Calm assumptions were inherent in their confidence, embedded in their psychological theories. Yet the working man resented being told that he was redundant, or that his friend was idle and dissolute, or that his union was social depravity, or that his poverty was a crime, or that his quest of release was a sin, or that his economic demands were unnatural. Carlyle saw it:

> Injustice, infidelity to truth and fact and Nature's order, being properly the one evil under the sun, and the feeling of injustice the one intolerable pain under the sun, our grand question as to the condition of these working men would be: Is it just? And first of all, What belief have they themselves formed about the justice of it? The words they promulgate are notable by way of answer; their actions are still more notable. Chartism with its pikes, Swing with his tinderbox, speak a most loud though inarticulate language. Glasgow Thuggery speaks aloud too, in a language we may well call infernal.[5]

The working class press spoke a language both loud and articulate; and, despite persecution and uncertain foundations, its influence as an educational force must have been very great, if for no other reason than its having actually attracted readers and hearers in significant numbers. It attracted those readers because it spoke to questions urgently at hand in a way both striking and just, no matter what errors might have been put forward.

When, in the developing reform agitation, middle class leaders and allies came to working class radical movements, they proved acceptable, because the impulses and watchwords were democratic and concerned with human dignity. After all, *The Rights of Man* was the manifesto of the age. Later, when the quarrels over the Revolution and the French wars had passed, and when the reform attained became evident for what it was, that alliance between classes was pretty effectively broken, and many former allies and leaders came to be denounced as truckling and self-interested. The metamorphosis of the word 'Whig' in working class circles is significant. The break was widened and class feeling exacerbated by the great popularity among the middle classes of their new dogmas, particularly that of political economy, which their publicists felt impelled to preach to the working classes. In the thirties and forties there was a real class struggle, evident to all.

From the end of the forties effective middle class allies reappeared on the scene—heralded most notably perhaps by the Christian Socialists—brought to understanding and enthusiasm by the impact of misery and by broad contact with the working classes. Modern political movements among the working classes have been shaped by their presence. In their concern and their goodwill they were perhaps not far removed from their counterparts of the twenties, thirties, and forties; but they no longer tried so hard to convert the working classes to middle class theories. They themselves became gradually assimilated to the working class point of view, and so were 'traitors to their class.' Representatives of such a trend are discernible in the earlier period; in a few persons, such as Owen or O'Connor, it is marked; but these traces are distinctly exceptional to the generally buoyant and self-confident approach of these decades. Then even the radicals were out to conquer; and that in later years they were conquered is a remarkable factor in the significance of that cluster of puzzling years for which 1848 stands as the traditional symbol.

A NOTE ON SOURCES

Following is a list of manuscript sources used: In the British Museum, my heaviest reliance was on the Place papers, but the Hone papers and the Correspondence of the Chartist Convention provided some information of value. In addition, the British Museum has in the Reading Room a collection of documents, mostly printed committee minutes, dealing with the Society for the Diffusion of Useful Knowledge; it is cited in the notes as S.D.U.K., Ellis Collection. The chief source for the S.D.U.K. was the collection of papers in the library of University College, London: 2 boxes of Baldwin Correspondence, 1 box of Special Topics, and 14 boxes of Letters. For the S.P.C.K. I used the minutes in S.P.C.K. House, London. The Appendix to the Minutes of the Manchester Statistical Society, 1833-43, in the Central Reference Library, Manchester; and Nassau Senior's Account of the Poor Law Amendment Bill, MS. No. 173 in the Goldsmiths' Library were also useful. I also made use of the Robert Chambers MSS., in the possession of Mr. A. S. Chambers, London, and Mrs. R. S. Chambers, Balerno, Midlothian; and the Tremenheere MSS., in the possession of Mr. C. W. Borlase Parker, Penzance.

Most of the broadsides, pamphlets, and little books which are cited can be found in either the British Museum or the Goldsmiths' Library of the University of London, but some material which I found in other libraries may not be duplicated in the London collections. This applies chiefly to local publications. Following is a list of the other libraries in which I worked: Central Reference Library, Birmingham; Edinburgh Room, Public Library, Edinburgh; New College Library, Edinburgh; National Library of Scotland, Edinburgh; Mitchell Library, Glasgow; Central Reference Library, Leeds; Central Reference Library, Manchester; John Rylands Library, Manchester; Central Reference Library, Newcastle-upon-Tyne; and the New York Public Library.

CHAPTER I

1. *Sphynx*, 9 April, 1828.

2. Add. MSS., 35,148/6-6b.

3. J. W. Adamson in *The Library*, 4th ser., x, 166-71 (September, 1929). Godfrey Davies, *The Early Stuarts* (Oxford, 1937), p. 356 and note.

4. *General Remarks on the State of the Poor, and Poor Laws* . . . (London, 1832), pp. 50-51.

5. P. Colquhoun, *A New and Appropriate System of Education for the Labouring People* . . . (London, 1806), pp. 12-13.

6. Alex. Christison, *The General Diffusion of Knowledge One Great Cause of the Prosperity of North Britain* (Edinburgh, 1802), pp. 9-11. Andrew Irvine, *Reflections on the Education of the Poor* . . . (London, 1815), p. 29.

7. *Parliamentary Debates*, n.s., ii, 56 (1820). *Quarterly Review*, xix, 97 (April, 1818).

8. Samuel Smiles, *The Education of the Working Classes* (Leeds, 1845), pp. 9-10.

9. *Journal of the Statistical Society of London*, ii, 98 (March, 1839). Joseph Fletcher, *Moral and Educational Statistics of England and Wales* (London, 1849).

10. G. R. Porter, 'Statistical Inquiries into the Social Conditions of the Working Classes,' Central Society of Education, *Papers*, ii, 261 (1838).

11. Compare Richard Watson, *Observations on Southey's 'Life of Wesley'* (London, 1821), pp. 152-55n.

12. A. E. Dobbs, *Education and Social Movements* (London, 1919), pp. 134-5, 208-10. Timothy Claxton, *Memoir of a Mechanic* (Boston, 1839), p. 16.

13. M. G. Jones, *The Charity School Movement* (Cambridge, 1938).

14. *Ibid.*, pp. 142-54. M. E. Sadler and J. W. Edwards in Education Department, *Special Reports on Educational Subjects*, ii (London, 1898), p. 438. Frederic Hill, *National Education* (London, 1836), i, 4-10.

15. William Roberts, *Memoirs of the Life and Correspondence of Mrs. Hannah More* (London, 1835), iii, 133, and iv, 180. Compare Abraham Watmough, *Observations on Teaching the Art of Writing in Sunday Schools* (Rochdale, 1832), and Joseph Barker, *Teaching*

the Children of the Poor to Write on the Sabbath Day, Proved to be in Perfect Agreement with the Word of God . . . (Manchester, 1837). See also Dobbs, *Education and Social Movements*, p. 148n.

16. Hill, *National Education*, i, 102. Rev. John M. Sinclair, ed., *Correspondence on the Subject of the Late Disturbances in the Manufacturing and Mining Districts* (London, 1842), pp. 15-16.

17. *S. C. on Education, Parliamentary Papers* [hereafter *P.P.*], 1835, vii, 54-58, Q. 643-96. *Reports on Education in Wales*, *P.P.*, 1847, xxvii, Part I, 3. Compare Dobbs, *Education and Social Movements*, pp. 74-6. Frederic Hill, *National Education*, i, 104.

18. Sadler and Edwards, *Special Reports*, ii, 446.

19. *S.C. on Education*, *P.P.*, 1834, ix, 20, Q. 262-7. Hill, *National Education*, i, 72, 90.

20. Sir Frederick Morton Eden, *The State of the Poor* (London, 1797), ii, 23. *Report on the Poor Laws*, *P.P.*, 1834, xxviii, 75, 79, 205, 644, and *passim*. J. W. Adamson, *English Education, 1789-1902* (Cambridge, 1930), p. 20.

21. Dobbs, *Education and Social Movements*, pp. 152-4.

22. *Report on the State of the Population in the Mining Districts*, *P.P.*, 1856, xviii, 24; 1846, xxiv, 14, 17, 44. Dobbs, *Education and Social Movements*, pp. 165-6. For an account of Tremenheere's work and an estimate of his importance to the social historian, see R. K. Webb, 'A Whig Inspector,' in a forthcoming number of the *Journal of Modern History*.

23. *P.P.*, 1849, xxii, 12.

24. *P.P.*, 1849, xxii, 9; 1847, xvi, 26; and 1846, xxiv, 13.

25. Dobbs, *Education and Social Movements*, pp. 89-90. Adamson, *English Education*, p. 23.

26. Sadler and Edwards, *Special Reports*, ii, 446-7.

27. L. J. Saunders, *Scottish Democracy, 1815-1840* (Edinburgh, 1950), pp. 241-303, gives an excellent description of the system.

28. Tremenheere, *Report*, *P.P.* 1852-3, xl, 18-19; 1852, xxi, 36-7. *Account of the Edinburgh Sessional School* . . . (Edinburgh, 1854), p. 37.

29. For the charges, see Tremenheere, *Report*, *P.P.*, 1856, xviii, 18-19; Thomas Hodgskin in the *Economist*, 22 September, 1849; W. Cooke Taylor, *Notes of a Tour in the Manufacturing Districts of Lancashire* (London, 1842), p. 133; J. L. and B. Hammond, *The Age of the Chartists* (London, 1930), pp. 209-10.

30. Hudson, *Adult Education*, pp. 94-5. *Chambers's Edinburgh Journal*, 14 March, 1846. R. F. Wearmouth, *Methodism and Working Class Movements* (London, 1937), pp. 120-1, 145-63, and his *Some Working Class Movements of the Nineteenth Century* (London, 1948), p. 142. *Lancashire and Yorkshire Co-operator*, 6 August, 1831, 7 January, 1832, 4 February, 1832.

31. James Lackington, *Memoirs* (London, 1791), pp. 30, 47-52. *Educational Statistics of the Highlands and Islands of Scotland* (Edinburgh, 1833), p. 24n. On 'petty itinerants' used by the S.P.C.K. in the Highlands in the eighteenth century, Jones, *Charity School Movement*, pp. 186-7.

32. John Freeman, *A Method of Teaching Adult Persons to Read* (London, 1813), pp. vii-ix. Hudson, *Adult Education*, p. 6.

33. A selection of the most revealing figures will be found in R. K. Webb, 'Working Class Readers in Early Victorian England,' *English Historical Review*, lxv, 333-51 (July, 1950), on which this passage is largely based.

34. E. G. Wakefield, *Popular Politics* (London, 1837): 'The result of all the teaching put together is, that about half, perhaps near three-quarters, of the English poor can read, and a tenth part of them write.' A survey in the *Penny Magazine*, 18 and 25 August, 1838, concludes that, of adults of all classes, 'less than one-half' could write, and 'less than three-quarters' read. See also James Hole, *Light, More Light!* (London, 1860), p. 92.

35. In seven parishes in Kent in 1837, of 145 children over 14, 84, about 58 per cent, could read and write, 61 could do neither. In the parish of Alderley, Cheshire, a year earlier, of 955 persons above eleven years of age, only 69 could not read; 266 could not write. Manchester Statistical Society, 'Appendix to the Minutes, 1833-43,' MS. volume in the Manchester Reference Library, pp. 92, 73. The Manchester figures given in T. S. Ashton, *Economic and Social Investigations in Manchester, 1833-1933* (London, 1934), pp.65-6, are clearly for an isolated bad instance easily offset by other areas. See also *Report of the Poor Law Commission*, P.P., 1834, xxxii, 347c, parish of Ford, Northumberland. *Evidence of Employers of Labourers on the Influence of Training and Education on the Value of Workmen . . .* (London, 1840), pp. 8-9. Hudson, *History of Adult Education*, p. 190. Dobbs, *Education and Social Movements*, pp. 52-3.

36. Saunders, *Scottish Democracy*, pp. 250-2, 261-79. On the urban situation, R. K. Webb, 'Literacy among the Working Classes

in Nineteenth Century Scotland,' *Scottish Historical Review*, xxxiii (October, 1954).

37. Lackington, *Memoirs*, p. 261.

38. *Hints on the Unlimited Diffusion of Useful Knowledge, at No Expense to the Reader, through the Medium of the Mercantile or Trading Classes* (Edinburgh, 1834).

39. H. A. Innis, *Political Economy and the Modern State* (Toronto 1946), pp. 37, 44-5. [James D. Burn], *The Language of the Walls* (Manchester, 1855), pp. 11-12. W. Weir, 'Advertisements,' in Charles Knight, ed., *London*, v, 33-9, 48.

40. 'On the Lyceum System in America,' *Central Society of Education, Papers*, ii, 204 (1838).

41. *Illustrations of Taxation* (London, 1835), v, p. 82. On reading in shops and bookstalls, see *Artizan's Miscellany* (Edinburgh), 25 June, 1831; *Chambers's Journal*, 12 November, 1842; Sidney Webb, "Reminiscences: iii,' *St. Martin's Review*, December, 1828, pp. 621-2.

42. *Some Account of the Life and Writings of Mrs. Trimmer* (London, 1825), pp. 54-6.

43. M. G. Jones, *Hannah More* (Cambridge, 1952), pp. 138-50.

44. Roberts, *Memoirs of Hannah More*, ii, 384, 430-1.

45. *Ibid.*, ii, 460-1. *S.C. on Education, P.P.*, 1835, vii, 85, Q.948-55.

46. *Christian Spectator*, 19 January, 1842, p. 9.

47. *Ibid.*, 21 February, 1844, pp. 17-18; 17 July, 1840, pp. 114-15.

48. *S.C. on Education, P.P.*, 1835, vii, 52, Q. 607. *Report of the Committee for Promoting the Establishment of Local Schools in Edinburgh* . . . (Edinburgh, 1824), pp. 29-30.

49. *Christian Spectator*, 21 January, 1846, pp. 100-1; 15 December, 1841, p. 7. S. G. Green, *The Story of the Religious Tract Society* (London, 1899), p. 8.

50. *Journal of the Statistical Society of London*, i, 457-8 (December, 1838); xi, 218 (August, 1848). E. G. Wakefield, *Popular Politics*, p. 7.

51. *Christian Spectator*, 19 June, 1839, p. 107. *Poor Man's Guardian*, 11 January, 1834.

52. S. G. Green, *The Working Classes of Great Britain* (London, 1850), pp. 115-17, 123-4.

53. *Athenaeum*, 2 January, 1828. [Charles Knight], 'The English Almanacs,' *London Magazine*, 3rd ser., ii, 591-606 (December, 1828).

54. W. H. Wickwar, *The Struggle for the Freedom of the Press* (London, 1928), p. 30, n. 6.

55. Knight to Coates, 26 June, 1828, Society for the Diffusion of Useful Knowledge Papers, Special Topics, Knight. A list of unstamped almanacs for sale at one shop appears in the *Poor Man's Guardian*, 25 October, 1834.

56. *Ibid.*, 30 November, 1833; *Anti-Corn-Law Almanack* for 1841 and *Anti-Bread-Tax Almanack* for 1842, both published in Manchester by Gadsby.

57. John Fraser, *The Humorous Chap-Books of Scotland* (New York, 1873), i, 113 and *passim*.

58. C. R. Cheney in *The Library*, 4th ser., xvii, 98-108 (June, 1936). Library of Harvard University, *Bibliographical Contributions*, No. 56 (1905).

59. Brougham in the National Association for the Promotion of Social Science, *Transactions*, ii, 34-5 (1858).

60. [Henry Mayhew], *London Labour and the London Poor* (London, 1864), i, 303-4, 308-9, 314, 333-4.

61. Henry Dunckley, *The Glory and Shame of Britain* (London, 1851), pp. 3-4. *The Cotton Metropolis*, in *Chambers's Repository of Instructive and Amusing Tracts*, No. 1 (Edinburgh, 1852), pp. 24-6. *S. C. on Newspaper Stamps*, P.P., 1851, xvii, 371-89, Q. 2474-2613.

62. Charles Knight, *Passages of a Working Life* (London, 1864), iii, 17.

63. Dobbs, *Education and Social Movements*, pp. 101-2.

64. Wickwar, *Struggle for the Freedom of the Press*, pp. 29-30.

65. W. Weir, in Knight, *London*, v, 337. C. D. Collett, *History of the Taxes on Knowledge* (London, 1899), i, 30.

66. Instances of circulation in individual parishes are given in *Journal of the Statistical Society of London*, v, 17-23 (February, 1843), xi, 216 (August, 1848). *S. C. on Newspaper Stamps*, P.P., 1851, xvii, 196, Q. 1214. A. Aspinall, *Politics and the Press* (London, 1949), pp. 17, 32. Cleave's advertisement is in *Working Man's Friend and Political Magazine*, 12 January, 1833. The estimate of the number of readers per copy is in Asa Briggs, *Press and Public in Early Nineteenth Century Birmingham* (Dugdale Society Occasional Papers No. 8, Oxford, 1949), pp. 16-17.

67. Cooke Taylor, *Notes of a Tour*, p. 132. J. H. Elliott, *The Moral and Political Evils of the Taxes on Knowledge* (London, 1830),

p. 6. *S.C. on Sale of Beer*, P.P., 1833, x, 224, Q. 3796. *S.C. on Newspaper Stamps*, P.P., 1851, xvii, 93, Q. 600. S. Maccoby in *Politica*, August, 1934, pp. 204-5.

68. *S.C. on Import Duties*, P.P., 1840, v, 209-13. Aspinall, *Politics and the Press*, p. 28. Advertisements in *Poor Man's Guardian*, 23 July, 1831 and 25 January, 1834; Place before the *S.C. on Education*, P.P., 1835, vii, 71, Q. 810; Viscount Ingestre, ed., *Meliora* (2nd ser., London, 1853), ii, 188. The numbers of establishments are given in *S.C. of the House of Lords on the Sale of Beer*, P.P., 1850, xviii, 10.

69. *Sphynx*, 21 May, 1828.

70. *S.C. on Education*, P.P., 1835, vii, 72, Q. 816, 818. *Chambers's Journal*, 23 November, 1844. Brougham suggests adoption of the practice in his *Practical Observations upon the Education of the People* (London, 1825), p. 8, but the reviewer in the *Quarterly*, xxxii, 425 (October, 1825), doubted that employers would concur.

71. Tremenheere, *Report*, P.P., 1846, xxiv, 25. *Spectator*, 26 November, 1831. On the 'pothouse oracle,' compare S. G. Green, *Working Classes of Great Britain* (London, 1850), p. 115.

CHAPTER II

1. E. R. Turner, 'The Excise Scheme of 1733,' *English Historical Review*, xlii, 38 (January, 1927). Dobbs, *Education and Social Movements*, pp. 121-2.

2. Add. MSS., 35,142/237.

3. *Parl. Hist.*, xxxi, 752-3, 840-2. H. McLachlan, ed., *Letters of Theophilus Lindsey* (Manchester, 1920), p. 132.

4. W. P. Hall, *British Radicalism* (New York, 1912), pp. 178-81. *State Trials*, xxiv, 1022, xxv, 85-6. Add. MSS., 27,812/44, 27,813/11-11b, 109b-110.

5. Hall, *British Radicalism*, pp. 84-93. M. D. Conway, *The Life of Thomas Paine* (New York, 1892), i, 284, 310, 329, 346.

6. M. D. Conway, ed., *The Writings of Thomas Paine* (New York, 1895), iii, 64-5. Cooper to Tooke, n.d., *State Trials*, xxv, 120.

7. John Aikin, *Annals of the Reign of King George the Third* (London, 1825), i, 449.

8. *State Trials*, xxv, 166-7, xxiv, 489.

9. *Parl. Hist.*, xxxi, 484, 775. *State Trials*, xxix, 401-4, 436-41, xxv, 91, 153-5. Add. MSS., 27,808/17, 27,812/40-40b, 27,813/ 92b. Manchester Constitutional Society, *Rules and Orders* (Manchester, 1790).

10. *State Trials*, xxiv, 745-8. Broadside 449a in the University of London Library, 'To the Poor of Norwich.'

11. Aikin, *Annals*, i, 648-9. *Parl. Hist.*, xxix, 1311, xxxii, 488.

12. *State Trials*, xxii, 381, xxiii, 1052. Dumas Malone, *The Public Life of Thomas Cooper* (New Haven, 1926), p. 53.

13. Conway, *Life of Paine*, i, 346. *State Trials*, xxiv, 1021. Add. MSS., 27,812/29b, 27,809/268.

14. *State Trials*, xxiv, 394-5, 410-11. Broadside in B.M. 648. c. 26 (11).

15. Conway, *Life of Paine*, i, 323.

16. A. Aspinall, *Politics and the Press*, pp. 152-3.

17. Conway, *Life of Paine*, i, 337-40. Roberts, *Memoirs of Hannah More*, ii, 289.

18. Jones, *Hannah More*, p. 134.

19. Roberts, *Memoirs of Hannah More*, ii, 340-4.

20. *Annual Register*, 1792, Appendix to the Chronicle, pp. 92-6. Society for Preserving Liberty and Property against Republicans and Levellers, *Association Papers* (London, 1793), p. iv.

21. *Ibid., passim*. The Birmingham group reprinted a London pamphlet, *Equality as Consistent with the British Constitution* and a pamphlet of the Lichfield Association, *A Plain Caution to Every Honest Englishman. Address Congratulatory to the Friends of Government by a Burgher of Edinburgh* (Edinburgh, 1792?). *A Collection of Publications . . . of the Glasgow Constitutional Association* (Glasgow, 1793). Other Scottish examples can be found in vol. 52 of the Stirling pamphlets in the Mitchell Library, Glasgow, and in pamphlet volume Ca 32 in the New College Library, Edinburgh. The organization of the Manchester unit is announced in a broadside in the Central Reference Library, Manchester, and see also the Manchester tract, probably of 1793, *Minutes of a Conversation at the Monday Night's Club* . . . and a broadside dialogue between Mr. Bluster and John Bull.

22. The finest collection of Nott pamphlets was destroyed by fire in the seventies of the last century. The Birmingham Reference

Library has two volumes of them, indexed in the catalogue of the local collection, and there are a good number of them in the British Museum. On the identification of the authors, see the catalogue; *Local Notes and Queries* (Birmingham), 7 August, 1869, in the Birmingham Library; J. A. Langford, *A Century of Birmingham Life* (Birmingham, 1868), ii, 109-10, 117.

23. *Serious Considerations, Addressed to British Labourers and Mechanics, at the Present Crisis* (London, 1803). *Important Considerations for the People of this Kingdom* (London, 1803). *An Address to the Mechanics, Artificers, Manufacturers, and Labourers of England;* Publicola's *Addresses to the People of England; to the Soldiers; and to the Sailors;* and *An English Taylor Equal to Two French Grenadiers* . . . (a dialogue) were published by J. Ginger, Piccadilly. A Manchester broadside urging defence against invasion and praising the constitution, headed 'To the People of England,' and subscribed 'An Englishman of the Old Sort,' is in the Central Reference Library, Manchester. The Rylands Library contains five numbers of *The Invasion*, published in Glasgow in 1803; each number has eight pages and sold for a halfpenny or fourpence per dozen for distribution.

24. Mention should be made of the plan submitted by one William Playfair to the Home Office in 1794, reprinted in Aspinall, *Politics and the Press*, pp. 436-8.

25. J. L. and B. Hammond, *The Town Labourer, 1760-1832* (London, 1917), p. 288. Place to W. E. Hickson, 6 November, 1843. Add. MSS., 35,151/369b.

26. *A Correct Report of . . . the Trial of Thirty-eight Men, on a Charge of Administering an Unlawful Oath . . . at Lancaster . . .* (Manchester, 1812), pp. 84, 102.

27. *Quarterly Review*, viii, 347-9 (December, 1812). A. Aspinall, *The Early English Trade Unions* (London, 1949), pp. 31, 174. King v. Mellar and others, 6 January, *Report of Proceedings under Commissions of Oyer and Terminer and Gaol Delivery for the County of York* . . . (London, 1813), p. 39.

28. Aspinall, *Trade Unions*, p. 352. See also in the Central Reference Library, Manchester, the huge broadside headed 'Fellow Weavers' and subscribed 'An Old Weaver,' an appeal against machine-breaking; and the pamphlets, with identification of authorship by W. R. Hay, in 329.2/T1.

29. Davis, *Age of Grey and Peel*, p. 173. Knight, *Passages of a Working Life*, i, 128-37, 162.

30. *Parl. Deb.*, xxiii, 951-5, 1029-39.

31. *Parl. Deb.*, xxxv, 411-19, 438-47.

32. *Parl. Deb.*, xxxv, 554, 572-3, 621; xli, 1583.

33. *Parl. Deb.*, xli, 982, 1354, 377.

34. *A Letter to Earl Fitzwilliam . . . by a Member of No Party* (London, 1819), pp. 47-50. Rev. Lionel Thomas Bergner, *A Warning Letter to His Royal Highness the Prince Regent* (London, 1819), pp. 27-9. Aspinall, *Trade Unions*, pp. 243-4, 257, 288, 336.

35. *Republican*, vii, 683, and v, 280 sqq., quoted in W. H. Wickwar, *Struggle for the Freedom of the Press*, p. 69. There is a catalogue of Carlile's publications in the Goldsmiths' Library, dated 1819.

36. Wickwar, *Struggle for the Freedom of the Press*, p. 57. *Black Dwarf*, 8 April, 1818.

37. *Gorgon, passim.* Graham Wallas, *The Life of Francis Place* (London 1919), pp. 204-5. E. Halevy, *A History of the English People*, ii, 65. Wickwar, *Struggle for the Freedom of the Press*, p. 65. L. S. Marshall, *The Development of Public Opinion in Manchester, 1770-1820* (Syracuse, N.Y., 1946), pp. 149-50.

38. For example, *The British Constitution Triumphant; or, a Picture of the Radical Conclave. (The Loyalist's House That Jack Built)* (6th edn., London, 1820). Wickwar, *Struggle for the Freedom of the Press*, pp. 60-7.

39. Davis, *Age of Grey and Peel*, pp. 181, 184. *An Address to the Higher Classes in the Town of Manchester and the Vicinity. By an Inhabitant* (Manchester, 1820), pp. 9-13, 17-18.

40. Add. MSS., 35,153/96b-97, 106b. On local reading groups in various centres in the North of England, see Wearmouth, *Methodism and the Working Class Movements*, pp. 24-5, 88-9, 97-8, 111-12; and *Black Dwarf*, 8 October, 1817. The Newcastle pamphlets are in B.M. 8135. e.2. The Nottingham *Facts Tending to Prove . . . a Right to Annual Parliaments*, with an advertisement of other publications, is in the Central Library, Manchester. The local collection at Birmingham is excellent on this period.

41. Davis, *Age of Grey and Peel*, pp. 193-5. G. D. H. Cole, *The Life of William Cobbett* (London, 1924), p. 180.

42. *Political Register*, 16 November, 30 November, 1816, and *passim*. Alexander Bain, *James Mill* (London, 1882), p. 430n. Add. MSS., 27,809/17.

43. Marshall, *Public Opinion in Manchester*, p. 144. Samuel Bamford, *Passages in the Life of a Radical* (London, 1893), ii, 24-5. E. I. Carlyle, *William Cobbett* (London, 1904), p. 201.

44. *Westminster Review*, xxiii, 453 (October, 1835). Place's opinion in Add. MSS., 27,809/17.

45. *Poor Man's Guardian*, 10 August, 1833, and 26 October, 1833.

46. *The Times'* obituary, quoted in the *Poor Man's Guardian*, 27 June, 1835. *Athenaeum*, 12 February, 1828. *Poor Man's Advocate*, 15 September, 1832.

47. *Athenaeum*, 12 February, 1828.

48. See an interesting discussion of Cobbett's finances in Arnold M. Muirhead, 'Introduction to a Bibliography of William Cobbett,' *The Library*, 4th ser., xx, 16 (1940).

49. *Political Register*, 23 and 30 November and 7 December, 1816, 25 January, 1 February, 1817. Wearmouth, *Methodism and Working Class Movements*, p. 165. On attempts to hinder the circulation of radical papers, see *Black Dwarf*, 23 April, 14 May, and 6 August, 1817; 7 July, 1819, 23 August, 1820, 11 April, 1821. *Republican*, 17 September, 1819.

50. *Annual Register*, 1817, pp. 60-1.

51. *Political Register*, 5 April, 1817.

52. The attack continued to Cobbett's death. See *The Broken Gridiron; or, Cobbett in the Frying Pan, by a Mechanic* (Leeds, 1827); *Nice Pickings: A Countryman's Remarks on Cobbett's 'Letter to the King'* (London, 1830); *Cobbett's Penny Trash* (three numbers, London, February-April, 1831); *Cobbett's Reflections on Politics* and *Cobbett's Ten Cardinal Virtues* (Manchester, 1832); *The Beauties of Cobbett* (London, 1835), a republished pamphlet of the earlier period. Considerable information on the diffusion of this type of material can be found in Aspinall, *Politics and the Press*, pp. 155ff.

53. *Spirit of the Union* (Glasgow), 1 January, 1820.

54. *Remarks on Wooler and His Dwarf* (Newcastle, 1819), pp. 6-7.

55. [George Buxton], *The Political Quixote; or, the Adventures of the Renowned Don Blackibo Dwarfino, and His Trusty Squire, Seditiono* (London, 1820).

56. Anti-Infidel Committee, S.P.C.K. Papers, London.

57. Roberts, *Memoirs of Hannah More*, iv, 10-11, 4-6, 18.

58. These and other local productions can be found in the extensive

collections at the public library in Newcastle and in two volumes of pamphlets in the British Museum, 8135.aaa.18, and 8135.e.2.

59. Rev. Henry Duncan, *The Young South Country Weaver; or, a Journey to Glasgow: A Tale for the Radicals* (Edinburgh, 1821), pp. iii-iv.

60. See the tracts in Central Library, Manchester, 329.2/T1. Marshall, *Public Opinion in Manchester*, pp. 161-2. Archibald Prentice, *Historical Sketches and Personal Recollections of Manchester* (London, 1851), p. 430.

61. *Searcher*, 19 March and 23 April, 1817. *Birmingham Inspector*, 15 March, 29 March, 10 May, 1817. *Edmonds's Weekly Register*, 9 October, 1819.

CHAPTER III

1. *English Chartist Circular*, i, No. 40 (n.d.).

2. *Poor Man's Guardian*, 7 April, 1832. Compare J. C. Symons, *Outlines of Popular Economy* (London, 1840), p. 12: 'It may safely be stated, that a single large street in most populous towns contains more books now than existed in the whole place thirty or forty years ago.'

3. [Charles Knight], ' Education of the People,' *London Magazine*, 3rd ser., i, 12 (April, 1828). Samuel Smiles, *The Diffusion of Political Knowledge among the Working Classes* (Leeds, 1842), pp. 14-15. *Spectator*, 15 June and 20 July, 1839.

4. The *Standard* for 10 September, 1833, reprinted in *Poor Man's Guardian*, 21 September, 1833, and in Maccoby, *Politica*, August, 1834, pp. 203-4.

5. i, 144. Knight to Coates, 1832 (n.d.) S.D.U.K., Letters, 1832.

6. Bain, *Mill*, p. 365. An ingenious attempt to avoid the stamp law was 'Berthold's Political Handkerchief,' printed on cotton instead of paper. The subterfuge did not work, and a young man was committed for selling it. *Poor Man's Guardian*, 3 and 10 September, 1831.

7. W. E. Hickson, *Report on the Condition of the Handloom Weavers*, P.P., 1840, xxiv, 78; James Mitchell on Spitalfields, P.P., 1840, xxiii, 249. Add. MSS., 35,150/190b.

8. P.P., 1850, xxiii, 28; 1851, xxiii, 31-2; 1852-3, xl, 21-2. See also J. C. Symons, *Tactics for the Times* (London, 1849), p. 3.

9. James Mill, article on education for the supplement to the 4th, 5th, and 6th editions of the *Encyclopædia Britannica*, reprinted in *James and John Stuart Mill on Education*, ed. by F. A. Cavenagh (Cambridge, 1931), particularly pp. 61-2.

10. Hudson, *Adult Education*, is the best source. See also Dobbs, *Education and Social Movements*, pp. 170-84. For the foundation of the London Institution and the struggle for control between the Robertson-Hodgskin faction and the Place faction, see *Mechanics' Magazine, passim;* E. Halevy, *Thomas Hodgskin* (Paris, 1903), pp. 84-5; and Place's *ex parte* account, Add. MSS., 27,823/237-93. On the change in their character and their decline, see [B. F. Duppa,] *A Manual for Mechanics' Institutions* (London, 1839), pp. 114-15; James Hole, *An Essay on the History and Management of Literary, Scientific, and Mechanics' Institutions. . .* (London, 1853); *Herald to the Trades Advocate* (Glasgow), 16 October and 6 November, 1830. The quoted comment is from J. C. Symons, *Outlines of Popular Economy*, p. 46.

11. *Edinburgh Review*, xlv, 197 (December, 1826). James Simpson, *Necessity of Popular Education, as a National Object . . .* (Edinburgh, 1834), p. 234. *Adult Education: Being a Statement of the Principles and Objects of the Leeds Popular Instruction Society* (Leeds 1839). The MacKenzie prospectus is in a letter to Coates, 7 October, 1836, S.D.U.K., Letters.

12. *S.C. on Public Libraries*, P.P., 1849, xvii, 24, 80-3, 90, and *passim.* Hudson, *passim*, and Tremenheere's reports, *passim*, give much information on village and factory libraries. Some interesting figures on circulation of books and occupations of borrowers in Salford and Liverpool in the late fifties can be found in the National Association for the Promotion of Social Science, *Transactions*, i, 581-2, and ii, 694-5.

13. There is, for example, a pretty extravagant passage in G. D. H. Cole and Raymond Postgate, *The Common People* (London, 1947), pp. 310-11. The only large-scale attempt at an assessment of the Society's work is an unsatisfactory and unpublished dissertation in the University of London: M. C. Grobel, 'The Society for the Diffusion of Useful Knowledge, 1826-1846'.

14. The prospectus can be found in the British Museum, Press Mark 820.f.43.

15. Baldwin to Coates [December, 1829], S.D.U.K., Baldwin Correspondence. There is an excellent summary of the plan and

graded functions of the publications in the *Edinburgh Review*, vol. 50, 181-4 (October, 1829).

16. All the letters written on this tour are in the box marked Special Topics, Knight.

17. Baldwin to Coates [December, 1829], Baldwin Correspondence.

18. S.D.U.K., Ellis Collection in British Museum.

19. Bain, *Mill*, p. 366. ·

20. G. W. Pringle to Coates, 8 October, 1831, S.D.U.K., Letters. Baldwin Correspondence, 24 March, 1829 and 8 April, 1836. Ellis Collection, Minutes, 13 November, 1834. *Northern Star*, 28 March, 1840.

21. N. Morren to Coates, 10 April, 1840, S.D.U.K., Letters. Particularly galling to the Committee must have been the letter from Henry James, a Holborn bookseller, 19 February, 1828, indicating that some of the apprentices and errand boys he had persuaded to buy the treatises had announced their intention to discontinue and to take instead the *Mirror*, the *Mechanics' Register*, and so on; one took Cobbett's *Register*.

22. Minutes, 11 March, 1835, Ellis Collection; Minutes, 8 November, 1837, Baldwin Correspondence ; *Address of Committee, June 1, 1843* (London, 1843).

23. *Address of the Committee of the Society for the Diffusion of Useful Knowledge* (London, 1846), pp. 3-4.

24. *London Magazine*, 3rd ser., i, 6-7 (April, 1828).

25. See William Chambers's comments, *Historical Sketch of Popular Literature and Its Influence on Society* (Edinburgh, 1863), p. 11. Dobbs, *Education and Social Movements*, pp. 194-5.

26. W. O. B. Allen and Edmund McClure, *Two Hundred Years: the History of the Society for Promoting Christian Knowledge* (London 1898). This section has been based primarily on the minutes of the Committee of General Literature and Education, 1832-48, and the printed Reports of the Society, 1819-50, which include the catalogues of publications. Both are in the papers of the Society preserved in S.P.C.K. House, London.

27. *S.C. on Newspaper Stamps*, P.P., 1851, xvii, 385, Q. 2580.

28. Thomas Williams, *Means of Improving the Condition of the Poor in Morals and Happiness Considered* . . . (London, 1816), p. 60.

29. George Miller, *Latter Struggles in the Journey of My Life* (Edinburgh, 1833).

30. Knight, *Passages*, i, 225-6, 244, 246. *London Magazine*, i, 3 (April, 1828).

31. Chambers, *Historical Sketch*, p. 12. F. von Raumer, *England in 1835* (Philadelphia, 1836), pp. 139-40. *Family Herald*, 17 December, 1842.

32. Chambers, *Historical Sketch*, p. 11. William Chambers, *Story of a Long and Busy Life* (Edinburgh, 1882), p. 33. *Chambers's Journal*, 2 February, 1833, 4 January, 1845.

33. Lord Brougham, 'On the Diffusion of Knowledge,' National Association for the Promotion of Social Science, *Transactions*, ii, 25-42 (1858); Knight, *Passages*, ii, 179-84; S.D.U.K., Ellis Collection, Address of the Committee, 30 June, 1832; Alice A. Clowes, *Charles Knight, a Sketch* (London, 1892), pp. 225-6.

34. Minutes of the General Literature Committee, S.P.C.K. Papers, 4 June, 1833, 3 June, 1834, 17 February, 1836, and 7 January-1 April, 1837.

35. *Penny Magazine*, 31 March, 1832.

36. In the second volume of *Knight's Penny Magazine* (1846).

37. B. F. Duppa, *Manual for Mechanics' Institutions*, pp. 12-13. *S.C. on Newspaper Stamps*, P.P., 1851, xvii, 478, Q. 3248-51. *Reports of Assistant Hand Loom Weavers Commissioners*, P.P., 1840, xxiii, 323. J. C. Symons, *Outlines of Popular Economy*, p. 11.

38. G. J. Holyoake, *Sixty Years of an Agitator's Life* (London, 1892), i, 70, 77.

39. James Simpson, *The Philosophy of Education* (Edinburgh, 1836), p. 21. Collett's testimony is in *S.C. on Newspaper Stamps*, P.P., 1851, xvii, 151-2, Q. 923-7. *Parl. Deb.*, 3rd ser., xiii, 623-4 (14 June, 1832).

40. *Spectator*, 27 April and 4 May, 1833, 11 January, 1834; *Athenaeum*, 28 April, 1832. *Moral Reformer*, iii, 90-1 (March, 1833). *Fraser's Magazine*, xxi, 162 (February, 1840), on the other hand, referred to 'those nightmen and dustmen of literature and science, the Chamberses, etc., etc."

41. For criticisms, *Working Man's Friend*, 6 April, 1833; *Weavers' Journal* (Glasgow), 1 March, 1835; *Cleave's Police Gazette*, 30 July, 1836; *Cobbett's Magazine*, i, 364 (May, 1833). But G. W. M. Reynolds called William Chambers one of the best friends of the working classes; Chambers MSS., vol. 17.

42. *Penny Magazine*, Monthly Supplement for December, 1836.

43. *Poor Man's Guardian*, 14 April, 1832. The Hone identification is in Add. MSS., 40,120/371-5.

CHAPTER IV

1. Quoted in R. F. Wearmouth, *Some Working Class Movements of the Nineteenth Century* (London, 1948), p. 142. On similar societies, see *Poor Man's Guardian*, 18 January and 15 February, 1834, *Lancashire and Yorkshire Co-operator*, *passim*, Wilmot Horton, *Reform in 1839 and Reform in 1831* (London, 1839), pp. 44-5, *English Chartist Circular*, i, No. 48.

2. Rev. G. Wright, *Mischiefs Exposed. A Letter Addressed to Henry Brougham* (York, 1826), pp. 7-8, 10-11, 16-17.

3. *Suggestions Respecting the Political Education of the Lower Orders* (London, 1831).

4. James Kay-Shuttleworth, 'Manchester in 1832,' *Four Periods of Public Education* (London, 1862), p. 63. See also J. H. Elliott in *Evils of Taxes on Knowledge*, pp. 7-8. *Spectator*, 14 December, 1839.

5. Samuel Smiles, *Diffusion of Political Knowledge*, pp. 5-6, 17-18. S.D.U.K., *Report of the State of Literary, Scientific, and Mechanics' Institutions* (London, 1841), pp. 28-31.

6. Add. MSS., 35,146/54b: 'It is to publish two sheets periodically octavo double columns for sixpence, each number to contain a treatise on morals or politics, or political economy, or science. . . .'

7. *Edinburgh Review*, xlvi, 228 (June, 1827).

8. Add. MSS., 35,154/194.

9. N.d., S.D.U.K., Letters, 1832.

10. Anon. to the Committee, 12 April, 1831; a Friend to the Society to the Committee, Glasgow, 22 November, 1833, S.D.U.K., Letters. *Poor Man's Guardian*, 24 September, 1831. *Monthly Repository*, n.s., iv, 711 (October, 1830), vii, 376-7. John Wade, *History of the Middle and Working Classes* (London, 1833), p. 109.

11. *Birmingham Journal*, 30 June and 14 July, 1832. Broadside No. 529 in the University of London.

12. *Westminster Review*, xiv, 365-94 (April, 1831). I have been unable to identify the author.

13. Minutes of General Committee, 13 December, 1837, S.D.U.K., Baldwin Correspondence. Lord J. Russell to Coates, 31 August, 1842, in S.D.U.K., Letters, 1842-3. *Address*, 1846, p. 19.

14. William McCombie, ed., *Memoirs of Alexander Bethune* (Aberdeen, 1845), pp. 104-81. The little book is *Practical Economy, Explained and Enforced in a Series of Lectures* (Edinburgh, 1839). On the Bethunes, *D.N.B.*

15. *Companion to the Newspaper*, ii, 167-8 (August, 1834).

16. Add. MSS., 35,154/167-8.

17. Add. MSS., 35,154/162-95; 35,149/132-33; 35,150/173-4b.

18. *Conversations on the English Constitution* (London, 1828); G. C. Rapier, *Essay on the Polity of Different Species of Governments . . . to Which is Added, an Epitome of the British Constitution* (Newcastle, 1842); J. G. B., *Historical Essay on the Constitution and Government of England* (Newcastle, 1844); Richard Whately, *Introductory Lessons on the British Constitution* (London, 1854).

19. Tremenheere, *Report*, *P.P.*, 1850, xxiii, 54.

20. *Education of the Working Classes* (Leeds, 1845), p. 12.

21. Harriet Martineau to Tremenheere, 14 February, 1844, Tremenheere Papers.

22. J. R. McCulloch *A Discourse on the Rise, Progress, Peculiar Objects, and Importance of Political Economy* (Edinburgh, 1825), pp. 78-9.

CHAPTER V

1. See the report of a *Times* correspondent, dated 4 December, quoted in J. L. and B. Hammond, *The Village Labourer* (London, 1913), pp. 267-8. 'The fires originate either in private revenge, or are the acts of foreigners, and I believe of the Jesuits.' Henry Drummond to Place, 22 November, 1830, Add. MSS., 37,950/98b.

2. Hammond, *Village Labourer*, p. 284.

3. Hill, *National Education*, i, 110-11, quoting the poor law report, *P.P.*, 1834, xxvii, Pt. I, App. A, p. 264a.

4. *S.C. on Agriculture*, *P.P.*, 1833, v, 32.

5. *Fraser's Magazine*, ii, 572-3 (December, 1830).

6. *P.P.*, 1834, xxxiv.

7. See the opinions in the *Poor Law Report*, *P.P.*, 1834, xxviii, 206, 580, 597-8. Hammond, *Age of the Chartists*, pp. 149-61. *S.C. on the Sale of Beer*, *P.P.*, 1833, xv, 9, Q. 46; 13-14, Q. 118-23; 56, Q. 902; and 197, Q. 3349.

8. Hammond, *Village Labourer*, pp. 309, 318.

9. See also *An Address to the Men of Hawkhurst (Equally Applicable to the Men of Other Parishes) on Their Riotous Acts and Purposes* (London, 1830), a twelve-page pamphlet, priced at 2*d*. or 7*s*. for fifty, a second edition from Longmans; and Rev. Edward Feild, *An Address on the State of the Country, Read to the Inhabitants of Kidlington, in the Parish School-Room* (2nd edn., Oxford, 1830), 22 pages, for 2*d*. or 15*s*. per hundred. In Canon E. H. Goddard, comp., *Wiltshire Bibliography* (Salisbury, 1929), there is mention of *Common Prudence, a Letter Addressed to the Peasantry and Labourers of Wiltshire on the Incendiary Practices of Some of Their Numbers*, by the author of 'Common Sense,' an eight-page pamphlet.

10. *The Life and History of Swing, the Kent Rick-Burner, Written by Himself* (London, 1830), a pamphlet of twenty-four pages with a woodcut, sold at 3*d*. Carlile was not the author. *Prompter*, 8 January, 1831. *Westminster Review*, xiv, 210 (January, 1831).

11. [Francis Place], *An Essay on the State of the Country* (London, [1832]), p. 8.

12. *Westminster Review*, xv, 244-5 (July, 1831).

13. *S.C. on Newspaper Stamps*, P.P., 1851, xvii, 479, Q. 3253-5. Rick-burning was prevalent during distresses in the forties.

14. *State Trials*, n.s. (London, 1889), ii, 870-2.

15. *Address of the Committee*, 4 June, 1831, Appendix, p. xx. S.D.U.K., Ellis Collection.

16. S.D.U.K., Letters, Richard Moorsom to Coates, 14 December, 1830; John Tyrrell (a very active local member) to Coates, 19 December, 1830; James Mulleneux to Coates, 18 May, 1831; John Sheldrick to Coates, 16 December, 1830.

17. Ibid., Letters from T. W. and Arthur Hill, 19 December, 1830, two letters from B. H. Malkin, the younger, December, 1830; and one from B. H. Malkin, the elder, 25 December, 1830; Loch to Coates, 30 December, 1830. The 1830 boxes also contain requests from H. B. Ker for a Mr. Wingfield for a district in Essex; Alex Perry for Pembroke; Thomas Oakley of Preston, Herts, for districts in Bedfordshire and Cambridgeshire; Thomas Lewin for Elsham, and R. W. Rothman for Cambridge. See also *A Few Observations, Additional to Those Addressed to Labourers under the Authority of the Society for the Diffusion of Useful Knowledge* (London, n.d.), a four-page pamphlet printed by one Richard Taylor in Red Lion Court.

18. Knight, *Passages*, ii, 159-60. *Athenaeum*, 1 January, 1831.

19. Letters from B. H. Malkin, 25 December, 1830; John Trevor, 21 December, 1830; J. Starret, Belper, 1831.

20. *John Hopkins's Notions of Political Economy* (Boston, 1833), p. 141.

21. *Spectator*, 8 January, 1831. *Quarterly Review*, xlvi, 381-6 (January, 1832).

22. *The Reply of the Journeymen Bookbinders, to Remarks on a Memorial Addressed to Their Employers* . . . (London, 1831).

23. Birmingham *Journal*, 30 June, 1832.

24. *Spectator*, 20 November, 1841.

25. S.D.U.K., Letters, J. H. Moggridge, Woodfield, near Newport, to Coates, received 15 September, 1831; Martin to the committee, 12 April, 1831.

26. Sidal Howes to Place, Add. MSS., 37,950/108-109b.

CHAPTER VI

1. [Edwin Chadwick], *Edinburgh Review*, lxiii, 495-6 (July, 1836).

2. H. L. Beales, 'The New Poor Law,' *History*, xv, 308-19 (January, 1931); and 'The Passing of the Poor Law,' *Political Quarterly*, xix, 312-22 (October-December, 1948).

3. S. and B. Webb, *English Poor Law History: Part II: The Last Hundred Years* (London, 1929), i, 72-82.

4. Nassau Senior, University of London MS. No. 173, p. 167.

5. Malthus, *Essay on Population* (6th edn.), ii, 319-20. Senior, University of London MS. No. 173, p. 54.

6. *Quarterly Review*, xxxii, 421 (October, 1825).

7. *Extracts from the Information Received by His Majesty's Commissioners, as to the Administration and Operation of the Poor Laws* (London, 1833). See notices of it in the *Quarterly Review*, vol. 50, 349 (January, 1834), and in *Cobbett's Magazine*, i, 559-74 (July, 1833) and ii, 73-82 (August, 1833).

8. *Edinburgh Review*, lxiii, 505 (July, 1836).

9. Knight, *Passages*, ii, 244.

10. *The Poor Laws: Their Present Operation, and Their Proposed Amendment. Chiefly Drawn from the Evidence and Reports of the Poor-Law Commissioners* (London, 1834).

11. Harriet Martineau, *Autobiography* (2nd edn., London, 1877), i, 218-21. S.D.U.K., Ellis Collection, General Committee, 7 August, 1834.

12. S.D.U.K., Letters, 6 March and 28 August, 1833.

13. Richard Garnett, *The Life of W. J. Fox* (London, 1910), pp. 87-8. *Monthly Repository*, n.s., vii, 375-6.

14. S.D.U.K., Ellis Collection, General Committee, 13 November, 1834.

15. [N. W. Senior], *Remarks on the Opposition to the Poor Law Amendment Bill. By a Guardian* (London, 1841), pp. 43-4. Cecil Driver, *Tory Radical: the Life of Richard Oastler* (New York, 1946), p. 284.

16. *Companion to the Newspaper*, August, 1834.

17. 4 March, 1834, Add. MSS., 35,149/278.

18. *Political Register*, 8 March, 3 May, 12 July, 1834. *Poor Man's Guardian*, 8 November, 1834. Webb, *Poor Law History*, i, 153-64. Driver, *Tory Radical*, pp. 269-91, 331-44. G. R. Wythen Baxter, *The Book of the Bastiles* (London, 1841), *passim*. Lowery to the Convention, n.d., Add. MSS., 34,245A/120b.

19. University of London MS. No. 173, pp. 9-12.

20. Senior, *Remarks on the Opposition to the Poor Law Amendment Bill*, pp. 66-9.

21. Add. MSS., 35,149/311.

22. Some examples, primarily explanatory, are: Archer Clive, *A Few Words to the Poor and to Overseers, on the New Poor Law* (London, 1837), written by the rector of Solihull in October, 1836, for the poor of his own parish and republished by Charles Knight for wider circulation in the next year. *The Poor Man's Guide to Relief under the New Poor Law . . . by a Person Engaged under the New Law* (London, 1841), a Knight pamphlet of twelve pages at a penny and seven shillings per hundred. *The Poor Man's Hand-Book of the New Poor-Law, Being a Guide to Parochial Relief* (London, 1846), a fifty-page pamphlet published at threepence or fifteen shillings per hundred for distribution. There were also publications specifically for those who were to administer the new law; thus Maurice Swabey, *A Practical Explanation of the Duties of Parish Officers in Electing Guardians . . . and of the Duties of Guardians When Elected* (London, 1835); or *Instructions to Relieving Officers* ([Charlton Kings, Glos.], n.d.).

23. *Quarterly Review*, liii, 473-539 (April, 1835); Wythen Baxter, *Book of the Bastiles*, pp. 277-9; *Political Register*, 1 March, 1834.

24. Francis Close, *Pauperism Traced to Its True Sources by the Aid of Holy Scripture and Experience* (2nd edn., London, 1839).

25. Thomas Spencer, *The Successful Application of the New Poor Law to the Parish of Hinton Charterhouse* (London, 1836). Other pamphlets by Spencer and by many other clergymen as well are listed in Webb, *English Poor Law History*, i, 113, n.1.

26. Charles Wykeham Martin, *An Address to the Labourers of Egerton, in Kent, and the Adjoining Parishes* (London, 1835).

27. Rev. J. Bosworth, *The Contrast; or, the Operation of the Old Poor Laws Contrasted with the Recent Poor Law Amendment Act . . .* (London, 1838), p. 7.

28. Buckingham Poor Law Union, *Report by Mr. T. I. King of His Mission to the Manufacturing Districts, in Company with Edward Quainton, of Steeple Claydon,—and Benjamin Stevens, of Adstock* (Buckingham, [1835?]), a twelve-page, threepenny pamphlet. The technique is similar to that used extensively in emigration propaganda.

29. *Political Register*, 13 June, 1835. On Leslie, see S. E. Finer, *The Life and Times of Sir Edwin Chadwick* (London, 1952), pp. 356-8.

30. This review is in Oastler's cuttings on White Slavery in the Goldsmiths' Library. Other pamphlets of the same sort, addressed to the labouring classes and stressing the benefit intended by the framers of the new law to the working classes, and appealing to the respectable worker as against his idle neighbour are: *The Whole History and Mystery of the New Poor Law* (Bishops Stortford, 1835) a penny tract republished by Knight in 1840. *The Old and New Poor Law: Who Gains? and Who Loses? Explained by Conversations on Facts of Daily Occurrence* (London, 1835), a tiny dialogue. Rev. William Norris, *A Letter to the Inhabitants of the Parish of Warblington, Hants, on the New Poor Law, Its Origin and Intended Effect* (3rd edn., London, 1836), a sixpenny pamphlet printed in Chichester. Rev. J. N. Gurney, *The New Poor Law the Poor Man's Friend. A Plain Address to the Labouring Classes among His Parishioners* (Leicester, 1836), a six-penny tract by the curate of Lutterworth which appeared with a prefatory letter and appendix in a fourth edition in London in 1841, entitled *The New Poor Law Explained and Vindicated*. Rev. John Bourdier, *Remarks on Some of the More Prominent*

Features and the General Tendency of the New Poor Law Bill,
Addressed to Those Who Are Disposed to Think It a Harsh and
Oppressive Act (Warwick, 1837).

31. Knight, *Passages*, ii, 245-6. A catalogue can be found in volume
iii of the Poor Law Commission's *Official Circulars* (London,
1843).

32. *D.N.B.*, article 'John Latey.'

CHAPTER VII

1. Godfrey Lushington, 'Workmen and Trade Unions,' in
Questions for a Reformed Parliament (London, 1867), pp. 37-47.

2. G. D. H. Cole, 'A Study in British Trade Union History:
Attempts at ' "General Union" 1829-1834,' *International Review
for Social History*, iv, 359-462 (1938).

3. *Pioneer*, 19 October, 1833.

4. R. Torrens, *On Wages and Combinations* (London, 1834).

5. *Athenaeum*, 10 May, 1834. Francis Jeffrey, *Combinations of
Workmen* . . . (Edinburgh, 1825), p. 12. *Reformers' Gazette*
(Glasgow), 30 November, 1833. James Simpson, *Necessity of
Popular Education*, pp. 20-22.

6. S.D.U.K., Letters, Henry Gawler to Coates, 1 November,
1831. Gawler was Bellenden Ker's uncle and a member of the
Royal Commission on the Poor Law.

7. Ibid., Bartholomew Dillon to Coates, 28 January, 1832.

8. Ibid, Thomas Edgeworth to Coates, 17 March, 1832.

9. S.D.U.K., Ellis Collection, General Committee, 3 July, 1834.

10. S.D.U.K., Letters, Robert Christie to Coates, 5 March, 1833,
W. B. Baring to Coates, 7 and 26 March, 1833.

11. 7 December, 1833, Add. MSS., 35,149/242-4, 35,154/194.

12. Place knew that Knight was the author. It is credited to him
in Clowes, *Knight*, p. 256.

13. Add. MSS., 35,154/186-9; 35,149/245-46b, 247-9, 266b, 269,
281, 307b-308. The pamphlets are in manuscript in 27,834/4-145.
See also *S.C. on Education*, P.P., 1835, vii, 281-2, Q. 909; and
Graham Wallas, *The Life of Francis Place* (London, 1919),
pp. 354-6.

14. Martineau, *Autobiography*, iii, 95-6. S. J. Reid, *Life and Letters of the First Earl of Durham* (London, 1906), i, 343-5. C. W. New, *Lord Durham* (Oxford, 1929), pp. 237-9.

15. Add. MSS., 35,149/278-9.

16. *Athenaeum*, 10 May, 1834.

17. *Monthly Repository*, n.s., viii, 308.

18. See also Thomas Hopkins, *Wages: or, Masters and Workmen and Wages, No. II, (Shewing the Effects of High or Low Profits on Wages* (Manchester, 1831). University of London Broadside, No. 679a.

19. Add. MSS., 37,949/377, 378b. *Annals of the Royal Statistical Society, 1834-1934* (London, 1934), p. 44. *Journal of the Statistical Society of London*, i, 11-13, 50 (May, 1838).

20. *Chambers's Journal*, 23 June, 1838, 3 March, 1838.

21. James Simpson, *Brief Reports of Lectures Delivered to the Working Classes of Edinburgh, on the Means in Their Own Power of Improving Their Character and Condition* (Edinburgh, [1843-4]).

22. E. Welbourne, *The Miners' Unions of Northumberland and Durham* (Cambridge, 1923), pp. 60-81, esp. pp. 79-80. R. Fynes, *The Miners of Northumberland and Durham* (Sunderland, 1923, originally published 1873), pp. 49-117.

23. Welbourne, *Miners' Unions*, pp. 67, 74.

24. *P.P.*, 1846, xxiv, 7-8.

25. The volume is marked Coal Trade: Pitmen's Strike, 1844.

26. Harriet Martineau to Tremenheere, 25 January, 14, 19, and 23 February, 1844; Morton to Tremenheere, 26 February, 1844; R. Chambers to Tremenheere, 1 February, 1844, Tremenheere Papers, Family Letters, 1841-55.

CONCLUSION

1. 'Education of the People,' *London Magazine*, 3rd ser., i, 3 (April, 1828).

2. Knight's article in the *London Magazine*, 3rd ser., i, 6-7 (April, 1828); in a letter Knight wrote to Coates, November, 1831, S.D.U.K., Letters; and in S. G. Green, *Improvement of the Working Classes*, pp. 120-1.

3. *Westminster Review*, vii, 308-9 (April, 1827).
4. 'Poetry of the Poor,' *London Review*, i, 199-200 (April, 1835). Compare F. Engels, *Condition of the Working Class in England in 1844* (London, 1892), pp. 239-40.
5. Thomas Carlyle, *Chartism* (London, 1840), pp. 40-41.

INDEX